At Issue

Are Natural
Disasters Increasing?

Other Books in the At Issue Series:

Alcohol Abuse

Alternatives to Prisons

Are Adoption Policies Fair?

Are Books Becoming Extinct?

Are Executives Paid Too Much?

Are Government Bailouts Effective?

Are Women Paid Fairly?

Biofuels

Book Banning

Club Drugs

Distracted Driving

Does the World Hate the US?

Fracking

Guns and Crime

Should the Drinking Age Be Lowered?

Teen Residential Treatment Programs

What Is the Impact of Twitter?

At Issue

Are Natural Disasters Increasing?

Roman Espejo, Book Editor

GREENHAVEN PRESS
A part of Gale, Cengage Learning

GALE
CENGAGE Learning·

Farmington Hills, Mich • San Francisco • New York • Waterville, Maine
Meriden, Conn • Mason, Ohio • Chicago

Elizabeth Des Chenes, *Director, Content Strategy*
Cynthia Sanner, *Publisher*
Douglas Dentino, Manager, *New Product*

© 2014 Greenhaven Press, a part of Gale, Cengage Learning.

WCN: 01-100-101

Gale and Greenhaven Press are registered trademarks used herein under license.

For more information, contact:
Greenhaven Press
27500 Drake Rd.
Farmington Hills, MI 48331-3535
Or you can visit our Internet site at gale.cengage.com

For product information and technology assistance, contact us at

Gale Customer Support, 1-800-877-4253
For permission to use material from this text or product, submit all requests online at
www.cengage.com/permissions

Further permissions questions can be e-mailed to permissionrequest@cengage.com

Articles in Greenhaven Press anthologies are often edited for length to meet page requirements. In addition, original titles of these works are changed to clearly present the main thesis and to explicitly indicate the author's opinion. Every effort is made to ensure that Greenhaven Press accurately reflects the original intent of the authors. Every effort has been made to trace the owners of copyrighted material.

Cover photograph © Sue Poyton. Image from BigstockPhoto.com.

LIBRARY OF CONGRESS CATALOGING-IN-PUBLICATION DATA

Are natural disasters increasing? / Roman Espejo, book editor.
    pages cm. -- (At issue)
    Includes bibliographical references and index.
    ISBN 978-0-7377-6822-0 (hardcover) -- ISBN 978-0-7377-6823-7 (pbk.)
    1. Natural disasters. I. Espejo, Roman, 1977- II. Series: At issue. Disasters.
    GB5014.A75 2014
    363.34--dc23
                                                                2013042517

Printed in the United States of America
1 2 3 4 5 6 7 18 17 16 15 14

Contents

Introduction   7

1. Climate Change Is Increasing the Severity   11
   of Natural Disasters
   Andrew Freedman

2. Climate Change Is Increasing the Frequency   18
   of Floods and Droughts
   Paul A. Dirmeyer

3. Climate Change Is Not Increasing   27
   the Frequency of Floods
   Kenneth Artz

4. Natural Disasters Are Hitting Harder,   31
   and Not Because of Global Warming
   Jacey Fortin

5. Natural Disasters Caused by Human   40
   Activity Have Increased
   Brian Merchant

6. Urbanization Increases the Threat   45
   of Natural Disasters
   Stewart M. Patrick

7. The Increase of Natural Disasters   50
   Is a Biblical Prophecy
   Ron Fraser

8. Catastrophe on Camera: Why Media Coverage   56
   of Natural Disasters Is Flawed
   Patrick Cockburn

9. The Frequency of Earthquakes   64
   Is Not Increasing
   Colin Stark

10. Counting the Costs of Calamities   68
    Economist

11. Economic Recovery from Natural   78
    Disasters Is Declining
    Richard Heinberg

12. International Laws Fail to Address   84
    Disaster-Driven Migration
    Michael Clemens

Organizations to Contact   88

Bibliography   92

Index   97

Introduction

In geophysical terms, the earthquake that struck Japan on March 11, 2011, was mind-boggling. Measuring a magnitude of 9.0 on the Richter scale—the most powerful on record for the tremor-prone nation—it shifted Japan's main island east by eight feet and sunk two hundred fifty miles of its coastline by two feet. Additionally, it moved the planet on its axis by four inches and shortened the length of the day by 1.8 microseconds. In human terms, the earthquake was unimaginably devastating. It unleashed a tsunami that obliterated entire coastal cities with its thirty-foot waves—with surges up to six miles inland—killing more than nineteen thousand people and causing a major reactor meltdown at the Fukushima Daini Nuclear Power Station. Economically, the costs reached a record-breaking $300 billion, disrupting the production of semiconductors and automobiles, industries that drive Japan's economy. "I consider this earthquake and tsunami along with the current situation regarding the nuclear power plants to be in some regards the most severe crisis in the 65 years since the end of the Second World War," declared Japan's then-prime minister, Naoto Kan, in an official statement.[1]

The catastrophe in Japan evoked the devastation of the colossal Sumatra tsunami—the worst in human history—that ravaged several countries on the day after Christmas in 2004. It was triggered by a massive earthquake under the Indian Ocean that measured between 9.1 and 9.3, equivalent to the energy of twenty-three thousand atomic bombs. Waves set off by the tsunami reached heights of fifty feet in some areas and were forceful enough to uncover the ruins of an ancient Indian port city. According to the US Geological Survey (USGS), the death toll topped 227,000; Indonesia sustained the most

1. "Message from the Prime Minister," March 13, 2011. www.kantei.go.jp/foreign/kan/statement/201103/13message_e.html.

casualties by far at 130,000, followed by Sri Lanka, India, and Thailand. "The earthquake and tsunami brought to us the realization that many of our communities are vulnerable to natural hazards, and that such vulnerability is heightened as long as development investment in those communities do not appropriately consider disaster risks," stated Ong Keng Yong, then secretary-general of the Association of Southeast Asian Nations (ASEAN), at a conference in March 2005.[2]

In fact, the destructive tsunamis in Japan and Southeast Asia, which took place only seven years apart, have some experts claiming that the phenomenon is an underrated threat. "Many nations in the Indian Ocean did not even recognize the word 'tsunami' and none had tsunami preparedness programs in place," asserts Eddie Bernard, scientist emeritus and former director at the Pacific Marine Environmental Laboratory.[3] "Ignorance of the natural signs of a tsunami's presence led to inappropriate actions and decisions by nations, population centers, and tourist destinations." Bernard advises that the disasters should be a lesson to the world about tsunamis, even if the risks seem remote for many nations. "Tsunamis are inherently an international issue because destructive tsunamis do not recognize national boundaries," he points out. "In addition, tourists from other countries, including the US, suffered both casualties and injuries."

Even with a long history of tsunamis and an extensive warning system in place, Japan was cited for falling short in its preparation for a major one. For example, in a 2011 study of survivors living at shelters, Taiwan-based seismologist Masataka Ando found that many misunderstood how a tsunami behaves or when to evacuate after a warning. "About two-

2. "Remarks Delivered by H.E. Ong Keng Yong, Secretary-General of ASEAN at the Asian Leadership Conference 2005," March 3, 2005. www.asean.org/resources/2012 -02-10-08-47-56/speeches-statements-of-the-former-secretaries-general-of-asean/item /leadership-in-asia-after-tsunami.
3. *Tsunamis: Are We Underestimating the Risk?* National Academy of Sciences, 2012. http://nas-sites.org/revellelecture/files/2011/11/2012_Tsumani_Program.pdf.

thirds of the interviewees did not realize that a large tsunami would have struck them 30 to 40 minutes after the strong shaking stopped," says Ando, who continues that 10 percent did not think it would strike at all.[4] Furthermore, a United Nations nuclear safety team concluded that better planning could have averted the nuclear disaster at Fukushima. "The tsunami hazard for several sites was underestimated," observed the team.[5] "Nuclear plant designers and operators should appropriately evaluate and protect against the risks of all natural hazards, and should periodically update those assessments and assessment methodologies."

Still, it is proposed that the danger of tsunamis can be overrated. In a 2004 study of the Canary Islands, Russell Wynn and Doug Masson of the National Oceanography Centre in Southampton, England, determined that severe volcanic or landslide activity on the Spanish archipelago would not—as other scientists urgently predicted—generate a "mega-tsunami" with three hundred-foot high waves that would slam into the United Kingdom, Europe, Northern Africa, and the United States. "The mega-tsunami scenario . . . aired in the media is a hypothetical 'worst case,' and is largely based upon speculative computer models of landslide motion and tsunami generation," argues Wynn.[6] "Only by assembling all the facts and working together can we as scientists provide the public with the best information on these spectacular, but rather infrequent, natural hazards." Also, while warning systems have vastly improved with technology, they may miscalculate the forecast of a dangerous tsunami. "Following the 2010 Chilean earthquake, for example, scientists overestimated the tsunami

4. Quoted in Charles Q. Choi, "Tsunami Survivors: We Didn't Understand the Threat," LiveScience, November 29, 2011. www.livescience.com/30939-tsunami-survivors -understand-threat.html.
5. "IAEA Fact-Finding Team Completes Visit to Japan," International Atomic Energy Agency, June 1, 2011. www.iaea.org/newscenter/news/2011/japanmission.html.
6. ScienceDaily, "Canary Islands Landslides And Mega-Tsunamis: Should We Really Be Frightened?" August 19, 2004. http://www.sciencedaily.com/releases/2004/08 /040815234801.htm.

threat to Hawaii and the western Pacific because it took three hours for the tsunami to hit the closest DART (Deep-Ocean Assessment and Reporting of Tsunamis) buoy, delaying the time the scientists could use real information to refine their models," notes Jane Palmer, science writer for the Cooperative Institute for Research in Environmental Sciences (CIRES).[7]

Before the earthquake-spawned disasters in Japan and Southeast Asia, cataclysmic tsunamis seemed to be far in the past. The last one to claim upwards of a hundred thousand lives happened in 1908, caused by the Messina earthquake in Italy. Moreover, other calamities—hurricanes, typhoons, floods, droughts, and tornadoes—occur with relatively more frequency. *At Issue: Are Natural Disasters Increasing?* probes possible patterns in modern catastrophes and the trends that are thought to cause them, whether in the climate, the earth, or human activity.

7. "Eavesdropping on Tsunamis," cires.science.edu (accessed August 26, 2013). http:// cires.Colorado.edu/science/spheres/solidearth/tsunamis.html.

1

Climate Change Is Increasing the Severity of Natural Disasters

Andrew Freedman

Covering climate change and extreme weather, Andrew Freedman is a senior science writer for Climate Central, an independent research organization.

While scientists have not yet determined whether climate change increases the likelihood of extreme weather events, it is clear that it exacerbates their impacts. For instance, notable conditions set the stage for Hurricane Sandy, which battered the East Coast of the United States and broke records in October 2012. Higher sea temperatures and levels created heavier rainfall and raised the "launching pad" for a storm surge, resulting in the worst flooding ever seen in New York City's Lower Manhattan. Additionally, an unusual area of high pressure blocked Hurricane Sandy, forcing it to move in an uncharacteristic, devastating east-to-west direction. Some scientists claim that natural variability in weather patterns may have also come into play during Hurricane Sandy, but this storm raises urgent questions about climate change.

As officials [in late October 2012] begin the arduous task of pumping corrosive seawater out of New York City's subway system and try to restore power to lower Manhattan, and residents of the New Jersey Shore begin to take stock of the destruction, experts and political leaders are asking what Hurricane Sandy had to do with climate change. After all, the storm struck a region that has been hit hard by several rare extreme weather events in recent years, from Hurricane Irene [August 2011] to "Snowtober [October 2011]."

Scientists cannot yet answer the specific question of whether climate change made Hurricane Sandy more likely to occur, since such studies, known as detection and attribution research, take many months to complete. What is already clear, however, is that climate change very likely made Sandy's impacts worse than they otherwise would have been.

There are three different ways climate change might have influenced Sandy: through the effects of sea level rise; through abnormally warm sea surface temperatures; and possibly through an unusual weather pattern that some scientists think bore the fingerprint of rapidly disappearing Arctic sea ice.

Global warming-related sea level rise gave the surge a higher launching pad than it would have had a century ago, making it more damaging than it otherwise would have been.

If this were a criminal case, detectives would be treating global warming as a likely accomplice in the crime.

Warmer, Higher Seas

Water temperatures off the East Coast were unusually warm this summer—so much so that New England fisheries officials observed significant shifts northward in cold water fish such as cod. Sea surface temperatures off the Carolinas and Mid-Atlantic remained warm into the fall, offering an ideal energy source for Hurricane Sandy as it moved northward from the Caribbean. Typically, hurricanes cannot survive so far north during late October, since they require waters in the mid-to-upper 80 [degree]s Fahrenheit [F] to thrive.

Scientists said about 1°F out of the 5°F East Coast water temperature anomaly may have been due to manmade global warming. Warmer seas provide more water vapor for storms to tap into; that water vapor can later be wrung out as heavy rainfall, resulting in flooding.

The most damaging aspect of the storm was the massive storm surge that struck the coastline from Massachusetts to Maryland. Global warming-related sea level rise gave the surge a higher launching pad than it would have had a century ago, making it more damaging than it otherwise would have been. This is only going to get worse as sea level rise continues as a result of warming ocean waters and melting polar ice caps and glaciers.

The storm surge at The Battery [public park] in Lower Manhattan was the highest ever recorded at that location. It surpassed even the most pessimistic forecasts, with the maximum water level reaching 13.88 feet above the average of the daily lowest low tide of the month, known as Mean Lower Low Water, including a storm surge component of 9.23 feet. That broke the official record of 10.5 feet above Mean Lower Low Water set in 1960 during Hurricane Donna, as well as a record set during a hurricane in 1821.

Or, to put it in simpler terms, the water level reached 9.15 feet above the average high-tide line.

By warming the seas and the atmosphere, global warming is also expected to alter hurricane frequency and strength.

Katharine Hayhoe, a climate researcher at Texas Tech University in Lubbock, said manmade climate change likely contributed to the storm surge at The Battery in Lower Manhattan, with 15 inches of long-term sea level rise recorded at that location, the result of manmade sea level rise, sinking land, and ocean currents. She said the manmade contribution to the storm surge may have been a small amount.

But to the Metropolitan Transit Authority or Con Ed, the main electric utility in Manhattan, each inch of sea level rise matters a great deal.

If a similar storm were to strike New York in 2050, it would cause even more damage, since sea levels are expected to be considerably higher by midcentury. In fact, a recent study found that sea level rise has taken place at an accelerated rate at locations north of Norfolk, Va., and if this pace continues the Northeast could see much higher sea levels than other parts of the East Coast by midcentury.

A 2012 report by the U.N. [United Nations] Intergovernmental Panel on Climate Change (IPCC) found that sea level rise has likely increased extreme coastal high water events around the world.

Blocking patterns have been linked to several noteworthy extreme weather events, such as the deadly 2010 Russian heat wave and Pakistan floods, the 2003 European heat wave, and the March heat wave of 2012 in the U.S.

By warming the seas and the atmosphere, global warming is also expected to alter hurricane frequency and strength, making North Atlantic hurricanes slightly more powerful, while reducing the overall number of storms during coming decades. Detecting such changes in the observational record is difficult, considering the varying ways people have kept tabs on hurricanes prior to the era of hurricane hunter aircraft flights and satellite imagery. A recent study published in the *Proceedings of the National Academy of Sciences* found that warmer sea surface temperatures are tied to an increase in stronger Atlantic hurricanes.

"Blocked" Weather Pattern

In addition, an unusual weather pattern in the northern hemisphere steered the storm in an unprecedented direction, as it made a dramatic—and for many East Coast residents, catastrophic—left hook right into coastal New Jersey. The east-to-west movement, which is exactly the opposite of how weather systems normally move in this area, helped maximize the storm surge, since a strong easterly air flow struck the coast at a right angle.

The upper-air flow over the Atlantic Ocean was temporarily jammed by a powerful area of high pressure near Greenland and a storm system in the Central Atlantic, leaving the storm no escape route away from the U.S. Such patterns are known as "blocking" events, and they have occurred with increasing regularity and intensity in recent years. Blocking patterns have been linked to several noteworthy extreme weather events, such as the deadly 2010 Russian heat wave and Pakistan floods, the 2003 European heat wave, and the March heat wave of 2012 in the U.S.

In this case, the blocking pattern, occurred at precisely the wrong time—when a hurricane was moving out of the Caribbean.

Weather Channel hurricane expert Bryan Norcross wrote about this on Oct. 26 [2012]. "The freak part is that a hurricane happens to be in the right place in the world to get sucked into this doubled-back channel of air and pulled inland from the coast," he said. "And the double-freak part is that the upper-level wind, instead of weakening the storm and simply absorbing the moisture—which would be annoying enough—is merging with the tropical system to create a monstrous hybrid vortex. A combination of a hurricane and a nor'easter."

Some, though not all, scientists think the more frequent blocking events may be related to the loss of Arctic sea ice, which is one of the most visible consequences of manmade global warming. The 2012 sea ice melt season, which ended one month ago [September 2012], was extreme, with sea ice extent, volume, and other measures all hitting record lows. The loss of sea ice opens large expanses of open water, which then absorbs more of the incoming solar energy and adds heat and moisture to the atmosphere, thereby helping to alter weather patterns. Exactly how sub-Arctic weather patterns are changing as a result, however, is a subject of active research.

Some researchers who warn that climate change is already being felt in extreme weather events, such as Kevin Trenberth of the National Center for Atmospheric Research in Boulder, Colo., are not yet convinced of the Arctic connection. Others, such as Hayhoe, think it is a "plausible theory" that is worth investigating, although she noted there is evidence that Arctic warming may cause more blocking during the winter rather than during the fall.

James Overland, a scientist with the National Oceanic and Atmospheric Administration who recently published a study on how Arctic sea ice loss is altering the weather in the Far North, said it's not clear whether Hurricane Sandy was just a freak event or a sign of things to come. "What was highly unusual to me was the slowing down of the jet stream that normally turns hurricanes out to sea, allowing Sandy to directly [make] landfall," he said in an email conversation. Yet, he said it's important to recognize that there is still a huge role played by randomness, or chaos, in global weather patterns. "Having looked at a lot of weather maps, I don't think it's entirely legitimate to make a big possibility for an Arctic connection with Sandy rather than the chaos default," he said.

And while climate change has undoubtedly altered the background conditions in which all weather systems are born, scientists said that natural variability still plays a very large role, and may have been the dominant factor with Hurricane Sandy.

Martin Hoerling, a researcher at the Earth Systems Research Laboratory [ESRL], also in Boulder, is a proponent of this view. "Great events, like this meteorological one, can happen with little cause(s). Individually, neither the tropical storm nor the extratropical storm that embraced it, were unusual," he said via email. "What makes this a rare, perhaps once-in-a-lifetime event, is the fortuity of their timely ("untimely" as far as most are concerned who sit in harms way) intersection." Randall M. Dole, who is a colleague of Hoerling's at ESRL, noted that the blocking pattern that helped steer Sandy was "highly transient," which suggests to him that it was just "random bad luck" that it coincided with a hurricane along the East Coast.

Regardless of the chain of events that led to this disaster, Hurricane Sandy is almost certain to wind up being one of the top 10 costliest hurricanes on record, and it comes soon after Munich Re, a global insurance giant, warned of increasing natural disaster losses in the U.S., a trend the company said is related to global climate change.

And regardless of links between this particular storm and manmade climate change, Hurricane Sandy revealed many pressing questions. Like how much climate change is affecting storm impacts and extreme weather trends, and how vulnerable our coastal populations and infrastructure are to those changing risks. These are questions that political leaders, scientists, and engineers will be grappling with for many decades to come.

2

Climate Change Is Increasing the Frequency of Floods and Droughts

Paul A. Dirmeyer

Paul A. Dirmeyer is a research scientist at the Center for Ocean-Land-Atmosphere Studies in Calverton, Maryland.

Statistics and models demonstrate that disastrous floods and droughts are on the rise. The current body of evidence indicates that climate change is altering precipitation patterns, increasing the frequency of wet extremes in the United States and the rest of the world. At the same time, records corroborate a growing number of droughts driven by less precipitation. In the future, projections and simulations show that more periods of intense precipitation and dry days are highly likely. Mechanisms behind these trends are higher temperatures, including the increased capacity of air to hold water (leading to heavier rainfall and thermally unstable atmospheric conditions) and less moisture in the soil (leading to less rainfall due to reduced evaporation and the transfer of water from plants to the air).

Floods and droughts are among the most dangerous and costly of all natural disasters. According to statistics from the United Nations, during 1970–2005 over 30% of natural disasters were floods and nearly 15% were droughts or drought-related (wild fires and extreme high temperatures).

During the 30-year period 1980–2009, floods accounted for more deaths in the United States than hurricanes, tornados or lightning, ranking first among weather fatalities. Droughts are the main cause of agricultural distress, accounting for over $11 billion in damage in the United States during the first decade of this century.

Floods and droughts are not equal-but-opposite phenomena. Droughts are the absence of rain, and thus grow and retreat in severity at rates paced by the climatological ("normal") precipitation in an area. Droughts strongly impact agriculture, disrupting the annual harvest cycle, affecting prices for agricultural commodities in real time through market speculation, and, through lingering scarcities, rippling through regional and global economies for many months after the drought has ended. In some regions with decadal time scale climate variations, such as the southwestern United States or the Sahel in Africa, droughts can persist for many years or even decades. Floods, on the other hand, are caused by extreme excesses of precipitation or the sudden release of a surfeit of water from storage, such as a reservoir or snowpack. They tend to be more localized than droughts and rather short-lived, lasting hours to days, although large-scale floods can last weeks or months.

Although extremes in precipitation exist in the climate record on a variety of timescales, evidence is mounting that we are already witnessing the signature of human-influenced global warming in precipitation observations.

There is great concern that a changing climate brought about by the unprecedented human-driven changes to the composition of the atmosphere could increase the frequency or severity of droughts and floods. The latest report from the Intergovernmental Panel on Climate Change (IPCC) states that an increase in the frequency of extreme precipitation events is "very likely" to expand and the area of the globe affected by increased drought is "likely" to expand. In this article, we discuss historical trends in floods and drought, future projections, and the requirements of observations to monitor changes.

Historical Trends

There are numerous ways to define or categorize both floods and droughts. Meteorological floods and droughts are classified based on anomalies in precipitation. Hydrologic floods and droughts are measured in terms of deviations of streamflow or river water depth from historical norms. Agricultural floods and droughts are defined by their impact on crops and livestock. Other more specialized stake holders such as dam and reservoir operators, hydroelectric power concerns, river transportation networks and municipal water managers, to name a few, have their own criteria for defining floods and droughts. We will speak here primarily in terms of meteorological extremes based on anomalies from climatological annual cycles of precipitation.

Reliable raingauge data exist for much of the world beginning from the late 19th to mid-20th centuries, depending on the location. Satellite estimates can help fill gaps in the gauge network and provide estimates over oceans, but these estimates extend back only to the late 1970s. Records can be extended back in time in many areas using biological and geological proxies such as tree ring and pollen data, lake sediment samples and erosion patterns. These proxy methods are not as precise as instrumental measurements.

There exists in the Earth's climate a degree of natural variability on all time scales, and when speaking of variability in precipitation, the extremes are precisely what we call floods and droughts. These can be random chance events that reflect the chaotic aspects of the climate system. However, there are slowly-varying elements of the climate system that can enhance the likelihood of droughts or floods in any given year. Chief among these is the cycle of El Niño/La Niña events, a quasi-periodic oscillation of sea surface temperatures and oceanic heat content that is part of a coupled ocean-atmosphere mode of variability in the tropical central and eastern Pacific Ocean. El Niño affects precipitation variability on a 2–6 year cycle across much of the globe exacerbating drought or flood, depending on its phase, over Australia, Indonesia, much of North and South America, East and South Africa. It also interacts with the Asian monsoon system in a complicated fashion. On longer timescales there are variations such as the Pacific Decadal Oscillation and the Atlantic Multidecadal Oscillation that appear to be instrumental in driving long-term droughts such as the 1930's Dust Bowl over the western Great Plains of the United States, and the prolonged drought over the Sahel during the late 20th century. There is also growing evidence that the state of the land surface (e.g., anomalies in soil moisture) can act as a positive feedback, exacerbating both droughts and floods.

Projections indicate Southern Europe, North Africa, Mexico, the Caribbean, and a large portion of the United States and Canada will likely suffer dramatic increases in the incidence of drought.

Although extremes in precipitation exist in the climate record on a variety of timescales, evidence is mounting that we are already witnessing the signature of human-influenced global warming in precipitation observations. An upward trend in both the frequency and intensity of heavy precipitation events has been found over the United States during the 20th century. A subsequent study of global precipitation gauge records confirmed these positive trends in wet extremes over much of the world. Recently, a careful comparison to observations of multi-model projections of changes in extreme rainfall during the last half of the 20th century suggests that observed increases across more than half of the monitored areas of the Northern Hemisphere can be attributed to increases in greenhouse gases. Drought also appears to be on the increase over the last half century, driven not only by regional downward trends in precipitation, but also by the drying effect on soils of increasing temperatures and the change in timing of spring snowmelt.

Projections for the Future

A synthesis of climate model projections presented by the IPCC indicates an increase in both the occurrence of intense precipitation events (floods) and the number of dry days (droughts) over large portions of the globe, including many areas that may see significant increases in both extremes. To illustrate this, we show here recent findings using the global atmospheric model of the European Centre for Medium-Range Weather Forecasts (ECMWF). This model was run at a much higher spatial resolution than any of the climate models that contributed to the IPCC conclusions. Unlike those climate models, these simulations were made with specified observed ocean surface temperatures for the late 20th/early 21st century, and to simulate the projected warming those same ocean temperatures were added to the climate change signal from one of the IPCC model simulations in order to simulate late 21st century conditions (based on the A1b scenario for greenhouse gas emissions).

[The model] shows the projection for the change in the likelihood of summertime (June through August) precipitation falling in the lowest 10%, or a once-in-ten-year's drought based on the climate of the late 20th century simulation (1961–2007). Using that threshold as the definition of drought, we then compare to all summer seasons of the future scenario (2071–2117). "Double" means what was a once-in-ten-years drought is projected to double in frequency to once-in-five years. Likewise, "triple" and "quadruple" mean three and four times more likely. The large-scale features of the ECMWF model are in very close agreement with the official IPCC projections. Both projections indicate Southern Europe, North Africa, Mexico, the Caribbean, and a large portion of the United States and Canada will likely suffer dramatic increases in the incidence of drought. One should not read too much into the details of the small-scale structure apparent in this simulation (run at a spatial resolution of 16km [kilometers] or 10 miles). Rather the take-home message should be that there is a great deal of local-scale structure, and it is quite likely that over several decades, a specific location in the Midwest U.S., for instance, could experience much more drastic or mild effects than a locality 50 or 100 km away. The ECMWF model projections also indicate that over most land areas there will be a significant increase in the number of days with no rain.

"Gentle rains" are becoming less common. The greatest projected changes, however, are yet to come.

At the other end of the spectrum, there is also projected to be an increase in the number of days with heavy precipitation. [The model] shows the change in total precipitation in the five strongest flash floods—here defined as the five wettest 6-hour periods in the 47-year simulations of current versus future climate. Very few locations are projected to experience a decrease in extreme rainfall events, and large portions of the world are forecast to have 30% or more precipitation falling in those extreme events. Across much of the tropics and subtropics, increases of 100% or greater are common. These results are also very consistent with the conclusions of the IPCC for extreme precipitation events.

What Are the Mechanisms?

It is a fair question to ask, what are the mechanisms behind the changes in precipitation that all of these models project? First of all, the amount of water vapor that air can hold is a direct function of its temperature. That amount grows exponentially as air becomes warmer. . . . For a 1°C [Celsius] increase from the global mean surface air temperature (currently about 15°C), the capacity of the air to hold water vapor increases nearly 7%. The more moisture there is in the air, the more moisture can condense and fall as rain or snow. Global models and theoretical calculations indicate that the atmosphere conserves its overall relative humidity as the global mean temperature changes, so an increase in the amount of moisture in the air seems likely. Other factors may also contribute toward more vigorous precipitation, such as the fact that the lower atmosphere is warming faster than the middle or upper atmosphere over most of the globe. This causes the atmosphere to be more thermally unstable, and more conducive to triggering thunderstorms and convective precipitation. Factors such as these appear to be behind the tendency toward more floods.

On the other end of the spectrum, the tendency toward more frequent and prolonged drought also has several causes. Even with no change in mean precipitation, a shift towards greater percentages of rainfall coming in intense events would cause greater storm runoff and less infiltration of water into the ground. Coupling that with higher mean air temperatures leads to less moisture in the soil, which could have potentially disastrous consequences for agriculture. As mentioned earlier the state of the land surface, particularly soil moisture, seems to act as a reinforcing feedback to local and regional precipitation. Dry soils are accompanied by reduced evaporation and plant transpiration, leading to drier and more stable air that further inhibits convection and rainfall.

Conclusions and Observational Implications

Recent observations are corroborating the projections of climate models in terms of changes to the Earth's climate in response to the changing composition of the atmosphere driven by human industrial and agricultural practices. Most locations can expect an increase in the frequency and intensity of heavy precipitation events, and many locations can expect more frequent episodes of drought. "Gentle rains" are becoming less common. The greatest projected changes, however, are yet to come.

Many facets of the climate system remain poorly observed or not monitored at all. For example, soil moisture is currently monitored on a routine basis in at most a few hundred locations worldwide. Vast areas of the continents are hundreds if not more than a thousand kilometers from the nearest routine measurement site. Rain gauge networks in some countries are very dense, but in others they are unmaintained or nonexistent. Satellites offer the promise of routine global measurements of key aspects of the global water cycle, but all satellite instruments measure radiances in specific bands of the electromagnetic spectrum that must be processed and interpreted in terms of physical properties of the land and atmosphere. This is a complex and imprecise process. Furthermore, the average environmental satellite is in service for approximately 10 years, often replaced by a platform carrying different instrumentation that cannot be seamlessly cross-calibrated with previous data.

The result of such problems is uneven monitoring of the evolving climate of the Earth, and added uncertainty as to what is actually occurring and why. Long-term planning and support for global monitoring systems is needed—with perspectives well beyond specific field campaigns, satellite missions, or national networks. The design-build-operate cycle for instrumentation needs to occur with the time scales of climate change in mind—at least 50 years. Consistency in measurements is crucial for long-term monitoring. The more accurately we can measure changes in the Earth's hydrologic cycle, the better we can plan and prepare for mitigation and adaptation.

3

Climate Change Is Not Increasing the Frequency of Floods

Kenneth Artz

Based in Dallas, Texas, Kenneth Artz is a reporter for the Heartland Institute, a free-market research organization.

A new study refutes the alarmist claims that flooding is increasing in frequency due to climate change. An analysis of thirty years of data does not support such a trend, but finds a pattern of less intense floods instead. Moreover, while other studies do indicate a trend in more precipitation, they report that less extreme flooding events have occurred. What is concerning are populations moving into flood-prone areas, resulting in higher casualties and major property damage. Common misperceptions of increased flooding are spread by the vast and instantaneous media coverage of weather catastrophes all over the world and biased environmental journalists pushing a global-warming agenda.

A new study by scientists with the National Technical University in Athens, Greece, contradicts global warming alarmists' claims that flooding is increasing worldwide. The new study bolsters previous studies showing no global increase in peak streamflows.

Studies Find No Increase

The Greek researchers presented a paper at the European Geosciences Union (EGU) earlier this year [2011] and concluded, "Analysis of trends and of aggregated time series on climatic (30-year) scale does not indicate consistent trends worldwide. Despite common perception, in general, the detected trends are more negative (less intense floods in most recent years) than positive."

The new study confirms previous peer-reviewed studies finding little or no increase in flooding events as the planet has modestly warmed during the past century.

Scientists at the U.S. Geological Survey reported in a 1999 *Geophysical Research Letters* study that streamflow as a whole increased in the United States throughout the 20th century, but most of the increase occurred during low-flow and mid-flow events.

"Hydrologically, these results indicate that the conterminous U.S. is getting wetter, but less extreme," the study concluded.

A U.S. Geological Survey study published in March 2006 in the peer-reviewed *Journal of Hydrology* similarly found more precipitation but little or no increase in flooding events.

A National Oceanic and Atmospheric Administration study published in April 2009 in the *Journal of the American Water Resources Association* reported streamflow trends are rising during low-flow seasons, but there is no increase during high-flow seasons.

When there's a fire, hail storm, tornado or even a speck of dust falls somewhere, everyone hears about it.

Land Use Decisions Questioned

While flood events may not be increasing in frequency or intensity, the propensity of people to build in flood plains ensures flooding will remain a strong concern that will likely result in rising death tolls and property damage.

"The policies that make sense in response to floods and the threat of floods are well understood by the community of scholars and practitioners who deal with natural hazards. These lessons—such as building out of harm's way, avoiding reliance on structural mitigation when possible, the importance of shared public-private responses (e.g., insurance regimes), sharing risk and avoiding moral hazard, appreciating uncertainties, making good use of forecasts—are pretty insensitive to specific scientific studies on flood trends," Roger Pielke, Jr., professor of environmental studies at the University of Colorado at Boulder, told *Environment & Climate News*.

Media Changes Perceptions

Meteorologist Anthony Watts told *Environment & Climate News* greater access to media technology leads people to believe extreme weather events like flooding are increasing in frequency and intensity, even when no such increase occurs.

"In the 1960s through the 1980s, we relied on teletypes to disseminate the news. But in the 1980s things really started changing with the advent of satellite news. About 15 years later, the Internet began connecting everyone. The Internet was bigger than satellite TV because it was instantaneous and could reach everyone," said Watts.

"When there's a fire, hail storm, tornado or even a speck of dust falls somewhere, everyone hears about it," Watts explained.

H. Sterling Burnett, a senior fellow with the National Center for Policy Analysis agrees.

"Just go back and look at any American paper a hundred years ago: Would there be stories about children starving in Africa? No, because there would be no reporters there; for instance, the Dallas [Texas] paper a hundred years ago wasn't covering a tornado touching down in South Dakota. It just didn't warrant inclusion in the paper and there were no reporters sent there to cover the event the way we do today," explained Burnett.

Journalist Advocates

Adding to problem, Watts and Burnett observed, is many journalists have been corrupted by the idea of the 'noble cause' that justifies over-inflating global warming storylines.

"While some environmental journalists take the journalist part of their titles seriously, the fact that they are environmental journalists indicates the environment is something they have cared about. They don't see conflicts of interest because it's all in the pursuit of a good cause. Now we have a whole generation of journalists who are environmental advocates. They often check only with scientists whose views already match their preconception of the issue," said Burnett.

4

Natural Disasters Are Hitting Harder, and Not Because of Global Warming

Jacey Fortin

Jacey Fortin is a world politics reporter for the International Business Times.

Rather than global warming, infrastructural vulnerability worsens the impacts of natural disasters. The problem is most evident in developing countries with speedy economic growth, where populations are exploding, but safety regulations are lagging. For example, a 2012 typhoon that hit the Philippines killed over 1,100 and displaced 1.2 million people. In contrast, a typhoon of equal ferocity that landed in Japan that year only caused one death and minimal damage. Nonetheless, disaster risk management has not been a top priority for global organizations until recently, and attention spans and responses to natural disasters run short, prolonging devastation and recovery efforts in hard-hit regions.

If you've ever wondered what it's like to be in the middle of a massive typhoon, the first thing you should know is that it depends entirely on where you're standing.

"It can be terrifying, really," said James Reynolds, a storm chaser based in Hong Kong. He was on the Japanese island of Okinawa on the morning of Sept. 16, 2012, just as Typhoon

Sanba rolled in with maximum sustained winds of about 103 miles per hour and gusts reaching 127.

"We're talking about the wind screaming so loudly that if you were trying to shout at someone 10 meters away, they wouldn't be able to hear you," he said. "Rain so blinding you wouldn't even be able to see across the street. Waves crashing so large they inundated my location. When you're exposed to these elements you're deafened, you're blinded, water is getting everywhere and it's a very unpleasant experience if you're not prepared for it."

But Okinawa was prepared for it. There was only one Japanese fatality reported during that typhoon: The victim had gone for a swim at sea. Neighborhoods temporarily lost power and there was some flooding, but no major displacement. Only hours after the worst of the storm had passed, Reynolds was able to get in his car, drive down the highway and use the Internet at his hotel.

"I came through that whole experience unscathed, due to the fact that I was in Japan," Reynolds said. "I was in a sturdy building. If I had been in the Philippines, I'd have been in big trouble."

Less than three months later, Typhoon Bopha hit the Philippine island of Mindanao with sustained winds of 108 miles per hour and gusts up to 133—not much stronger than Sanba was at landfall. But this storm displaced 1.2 million families and killed at least 1,146 men, women and children.

Weather events of similar scale can have wildly divergent impacts from one country to the next—it's all a question of relative damage.

In these two scenarios, it wasn't the weather that made the difference—it was infrastructural vulnerability.

This preventable problem boils down to a single paradox: Some of the world's fastest-growing economies are finding themselves increasingly at risk, precisely because urban zones—with their high concentrations of people and economic assets—are swelling too quickly for safety regulations to keep up.

"Many cities, especially in developing countries, are very quickly expanding, and often expanding in hazard-prone areas," explained Francis Ghesquiere, manager for the World Bank's Disaster Risk Management Practice Group.

He noted that climate change has certainly led to an increase in adverse weather events. But the main reason economic costs of natural disasters have tripled over the last three decades? "First and foremost, the growth of population and assets."

Stormy Weather

Weather events of similar scale can have wildly divergent impacts from one country to the next—it's all a question of relative damage.

Two massive disasters serve as case in point: According to World Bank data, the earthquake and tsunami that hit Japan in 2011 resulted in losses of US$210 billion. The year before that, an earthquake in Haiti incurred losses of only about $7.8 billion.

But while Japan's disaster cost more in absolute economic terms, the Haitian tragedy was far more devastating in the long run—its $7.8 billion in damage amounted to 120 percent of GDP. Japan's earthquake, tsunami and nuclear meltdown combined cost only 4 percent of GDP.

The relatively high toll of natural disasters, combined with poor societies' inability to recover from them, puts developing countries at a distinct disadvantage.

A *Natural Hazards Risk Atlas* compiled this year by the London-based risk analysis firm Maplecroft ranks countries according to their exposure to risk, their economic liabilities and their resiliency.

Some of the data is unsurprising. The most resilient countries are those that enjoy high incomes and well-developed infrastructure: Japan, Australia, the United States, Norway. The countries that score poorly are ones that have been plagued by scourges like conflict, poverty and corruption: Somalia, Afghanistan, Yemen, the Democratic Republic of the Congo, among others. A single disaster in places like these can undermine years of progress by destroying infrastructure and siphoning off scarce resources in order to fund recovery efforts.

What's more surprising is that fast-growing economies—places such as Bangladesh, Vietnam and the Philippines (GDP growth for each topped 4.8 percent)—are actually the most at risk in terms of relative economic exposure, which is the value of economic assets that might be destroyed or compromised by a natural disaster, as a portion of GDP.

When Maplecroft ranked 195 countries in terms of relative economic exposure, the Philippines was listed as the most vulnerable country on earth. Bangladesh came in second and Vietnam was 12th.

The trend looks likely to continue as more and more small economies rev up.

"We've looked at countries which we believe have the greatest growth potential this year," said Helen Hodge, the associate director at Maplecroft who led the hazard risk research. "Those countries are accounting for substantial proportions of economic output. But those advances in economic output haven't yet translated into an improved climate for risk prevention over the years we've been investigating this issue."

As a result, developing nations are often caught off-guard when disaster strikes. International donors can usually be counted on to swoop in with some extra funds as global media outlets turn their cameras on the devastating aftermath and grieving survivors.

But this reactive approach is disruptive, inefficient, and far more costly than it has to be.

Blue Skies

For global organizations that make development their mission, one big question has been emerging in recent years: Why hasn't disaster risk management been a bigger part of the plan this whole time?

The World Bank got very serious about this problem in 2006 when it established the Global Facility for Disaster Reduction and Recovery, or GFDRR. Its goal is to help countries to lay down frameworks for development that include disaster risk management, which can avoid situations where poor countries go into shock each time a disaster hits.

"GFDRR is probably one of the fastest growing programs in the World Bank," said Ghesquiere, who runs the organization. "If you look at the number of staff, we may have had 20 to 30 staff focused on disaster risk management three to five years ago; we now have more than 130, and it's growing. It's also growing in the number of operations on the ground, with a lot of effort in helping local authorities better understand the risks to which they're exposed."

Once disasters fall out of people's minds and out of decision makers' agendas, the issue risks being sidelined.

Disaster risk management wonks gathered to discuss these ideas in July of last year in Sendai, Japan. The conference didn't make headlines, but it was one of the most important events the international development community has ever convened.

"[The Sendai Dialogue] is probably the first time that the topic was really brought to such a level of attention, to more than 150 delegations from ministries of finance, with both the World Bank and the IMF insisting that this is becoming a very serious problem that needs to be addressed in the long-term development planning process, not just in the response system," Ghesquiere said.

A comprehensive document called the *Sendai Report* was compiled in advance of the meeting; it outlined some of the key principles that now influence global efforts to keep development on track in emerging economies, come rain or come shine.

"The economic losses from disasters over the past 30 years are estimated at $3.5 trillion. Last year [2011] was the costliest on record, seeing estimated losses of around $380 billion," said the report, which urged a comprehensive approach to keep domestic governments fully engaged in disaster risk management indefinitely. Losing focus will be a constant danger, especially during those times when disasters fall from the headlines.

"Last year was, fortunately, one of the least deadly years on recent record for natural disasters—that's obviously great news," said Maplecroft's Helen Hodge.

"Part of the reason that occurred was because most of the major events we saw in 2012 were in developed countries. However, that does bring the risk of complacency. Once disasters fall out of people's minds and out of decision makers' agendas, the issue risks being sidelined."

Before climate change wreaks more havoc, development professionals hope to see the administrators of emerging economies set up programs that will help them face those risks head on.

As a severe weather reporter, Reynolds has seen that phenomenon firsthand.

"The main focus is always on Atlantic hurricanes; it always has been," he said. "And still to this day, when big storms pass through that region, that's where the main media focuses. I've been trying to report from the areas that have been traditionally underreported—to go there and be a one-man-band, so to speak."

But disasters in developing countries may be harder to ignore as they become more frequent, as they are likely to do as a result of climate change.

A November World Bank report notes that since pre-industrial times, average global temperatures have risen 0.8 degrees Celsius and sea levels have increased by 20 centimeters. Another 4 degrees of warming by the end of the century—a likely scenario, according to a growing consensus of scientists—will result in more intense storms, deadly droughts and famines, major floods and widespread disruptions of ecosystems.

But before climate change wreaks more havoc, development professionals hope to see the administrators of emerging economies set up programs that will help them face those risks head on.

Somewhere Over the Rainbow

International donor and media responses to disasters are still necessary to help fund recoveries, but history has shown that the follow-through can falter as attention spans run short. Calamities like Typhoon Bopha and the Haitian earthquake, for instance, are still ruining lives long after the news cycle has moved on.

In Haiti, more than 222,000 people died since the Jan. 2010 quake. Billions of aid dollars have been dispersed, but more than 300,000 people remain homeless. The food situation is insecure, and most people live in poverty.

In the Philippines, hundreds of people are still missing months after Bopha hit. Hundreds of thousands are displaced and living in tents and shelters. Tens of thousands are at risk of malnutrition.

Ghesquiere notes that the World Bank is working with the Philippines to establish stronger institutions that can respond more proactively to adverse weather events.

"Manila is highly susceptible to flooding, and so we've worked with the local authorities to design a large investment program to reduce this risk of floods, which is now finalized—an investment program over probably the next 10 to 20 years that is estimated at about $8 billion of investments," he said.

"Countries tend to, unfortunately, learn from disaster. The Philippines has had its fair share of adverse natural events in recent years, and you can see the system certainly coming together and the response system improving."

If all goes well, this could be the beginning of a success story—like Japan, which has worked for decades to minimize risks. The earthquake and tsunami disaster was a tragic one that killed more than 20,000 people, but it is worth noting that early warning systems were in place, hundreds of thousands of people were evacuated in time and troops were on the ground within hours of the incident.

"I think we don't give enough credit to the Japanese authorities," Ghesquiere said.

"You have to realize that reaching this level of business standards is not done overnight. It has taken 150 years for Japan to change its building [methods] and to have an infrastructure that can sustain this kind of tremor."

If the same kinds of institutional changes can be implemented around the world, perhaps rainy countries could gain the right tools to avert flood damage, drought-prone regions could avoid exacerbated famine, and communities near fault lines could build structures to withstand major quakes.

Hodge notes that this is a long-term goal—progress would come in stages.

"Being able to forecast storms is one of those steps toward building resilience that can be done on a swifter timescale, whereas improving infrastructure, improving building codes and enforcing them takes a little more time."

In an ideal world, these sorts of measures would work side-by-side with industrialized countries' efforts to cut down on their outsized contribution to the warming of our shared atmosphere. It'd be a win-win for everybody—the antidote to years of tragic losses.

5

Natural Disasters Caused by Human Activity Have Increased

Brian Merchant

Based in Brooklyn, New York, Brian Merchant is a writer and contributing editor for the sustainability website TreeHugger.

"Natural manmade disasters" are increasing. In these particular catastrophes, human-related activity and factors such as the growing reliance on technology, increasing levels of global pollution, and climate change are the main—yet preventable—causes and factors. Examples throughout history include London's Great Smog of 1952 when coal pollution choked the city during a windless cold spell; the Dust Bowl of the 1930s that occurred after farmers failed to rotate crops for decades; and when Hurricane Katrina hit in 2005 and levees failed to protect the low-lying city of New Orleans, Louisiana. In the future, more natural manmade disasters are imminent as failure-prone technologies are adopted and populations grow, affecting the earth's ecology.

An investigative commission called the meltdown at Fukushima [Daini Nuclear Power Station in Japan in 2011 following an earthquake and tsunami] an entirely preventable "manmade" disaster, and the media blew up. Any editor or reporter worth his salt in sensationalist muckraking, after all, knows nuclear disaster stories get eyeballs. The story goes: this was good ol' fashioned regulatory capture, the fox watching the hen house. A failure of government, a case of brazen reck-lessness from the nuclear industry—this was no freak fluke of nature. This was a disaster that could have been avoided alto-gether. This catastrophe was manmade.

Well, obviously. I can't really imagine a less surprising conclusion. The point of the investigation's revelation is to highlight the collusion between the government watchdogs and the plant operators, but let's go macro. The moment man builds a nuclear power plant along one of the most active fault lines in the world, he is guaranteeing that should a disas-ter strike it, it will be manmade.

There's no such thing as a natural disaster anymore a wise man who has been SEO [search engine optimization]-spammed out of history once said. The quote has been ap-plied to the earthquake in Haiti [2010], to Hurricane Katrina [2005], to other "natural disasters" that wrought destruction in a decidedly manmade manner. And it's true, to a point. Even the most organic, seemingly unpreventable disasters—nobody has figured out a way to keep the tectonic plates from sliding around—clearly wreak havoc based on how they influ-ence the manmade environment. But there's a new shade of ambiguity on the rise: Are these natural-cum-manmade disas-ters genuinely and actually "preventable"?

Of course, we have a slew of explicitly human-caused di-sasters under our belts—the Union Carbide gas leak at Bhopal [1984], our interminable parade of oil spills, our dam failures, the Love Canal [1978], Seveso [1976], Chernobyl [1986], etc, etc—but our history is lined also with manmade disasters that rode in on nature's coattails. These "natural manmade disas-ters" in the vein of Fukushima are only likely to grow more frequent as we continue to rely more heavily on technology, pollute vaster swaths of the planet, and experiment with the climate itself. So let's get acquainted with some of history's natural manmade disasters, to prepare for a future full of them:

London's Great Smog of '52

Here's a fine example. In 1952, unusually cold weather combined with an anticyclone and windless conditions to coat the heavily polluted city in a layer of smog. It blanketed the streets, looked like "pea soup" fog, and killed 4,000 people. A hundred thousand people fell ill, and research eventually concluded that 12,000 died as a direct result of the event. The cold spell was at the heart of the disaster, but again, it was the energy source that did folks in—as it got colder, they shoveled more coal into the furnace to keep warm, exacerbating the miasma of pollution that choked London.

In short, man made a city below sea level in hurricane territory, relied on technology to keep nature out, and failed. Sounds like a manmade natural disaster to me.

The Dust Bowl

After decades of farming without bothering to rotate crops, farmers across the Great Plains had depleted the nation's topsoil rather thoroughly. So, when the major drought of the 1930s struck, drying out the land, there was nothing to keep all that dust on the ground. So it created one of the biggest ecological disasters in US history, the Dust Bowl. Dust storms consumed entire communities from the South to the Midwest and forced millions to relocate and to inspire *The Grapes of Wrath*.

Hurricane Katrina

The greatest natural disaster to hit the United States in recent years might not be exactly that. Scientists have speculated that climate change might have been responsible for giving [Hurricane] Katrina the extra juice it needed to become a full-bore catastrophe. Kenneth Trenberth, a climate scientist and a lead author of the IPCC's [Intergovernmental Panel on Climate Change] 4th Assessment [Report] of *Climate Change [2007]*, has described it thusly:

"This is not to say Katrina was due to global warming . . . There is an influence of global warming, something like an 8 per cent influence. So if about 305 millimetres of rain falls in New Orleans [Louisiana] that means about an extra 25.4mm of rainfall more than might have occurred anyway. Often it's the straw that broke the camel's back. Was 25.4mm of extra rainfall enough to cause the levees to break?"

Scientists now believe that rising temperatures may be making hurricanes more intense (though perhaps less frequent). No scientist would ever say that global warming *caused* the destruction wrought by Katrina, but it likely made matters worse. Also, New Orleans had levees that were supposed to be able to withstand Katrina-scale wrath; design and operational flaws led to its failure. In short, man made a city below sea level in hurricane territory, relied on technology to keep nature out, and failed. Sounds like a manmade natural disaster to me.

Russia's Heat Wave

As with Katrina, we have to consider the same kind of climate inputs for the Russian heatwave of 2010, which killed over 56,000 people. Climate scientists worry that rising global temperatures fueled the extreme weather, and helped turn the event into a full-scale disaster.

Human civilization is now so enmeshed with nature that we can no longer honestly blame its whims for bringing suffering and destruction to our doorstep.

Earthquakes

The deadliest earthquake in recorded history hit China in 1556 and it killed some 800,000 people. Hundreds of thousands of people were living in dwellings built into artificial caves; the quake caused a landslide that wiped them all away. That might have been filed away as a natural disaster, but today, we know so much more about earthquakes and how to mitigate their impacts that our failure to prepare for them seems to place the ball more squarely in our court.

For instance, the devastating earthquake in Haiti annihilated its cities; shoddily built homes collapsed everywhere and left 50,000–80,000 people dead. So was this disaster then manmade? Man built the infrastructure that caved in upon him, after all. But it's a thornier question: In this case, it's really poverty that killed so many Haitians—Japan's comparative wealth and better building codes severely limited the death toll when it was hit with a comparable quake.

Of course, by heading down this road, we're forever blurring the distinction between natural and manmade disasters—a natural progression given our expansive adoption of failure-prone technology, our tendency to build societies that depend on it, and still-booming population that is transforming more and more of the earth's ecology. We've built cities that rely on air conditioning, for example; and if a storm knocks out the power, people perish. And that heat very well may be of the record-setting variety, given the greenhouse gas pollution we've pumped into the atmosphere.

You get the point. Human civilization is now so enmeshed with nature that we can no longer honestly blame its whims for bringing suffering and destruction to our doorstep. Nature is over now; we're nature. The planet is an ornery asshole but so are we; with each catastrophe we see our shortcomings and hubris reflected in the rubble. But I'm not sure we're stopping to take many notes.

6

Urbanization Increases the Threat of Natural Disasters

Stewart M. Patrick

Stewart M. Patrick is a senior fellow and director of the International Institutions and Global Governance Program at the Council on Foreign Relations.

As urbanization grows at an unprecedented pace, so do the threats of natural disasters to the world's largest cities. From 1900 to 2011, the number of people affected by fires, floods, landslides, and other catastrophes has increased exponentially, from a few million to three hundred million. Moreover, the largest cities are located on low-lying coasts, vulnerable to rising sea levels due to climate change, in addition to storms and tsunamis. The threat of natural disasters is not only contained to developing countries, as seen with Hurricane Katrina in 2005 in the United States and massive 2011 earthquake in Japan. Therefore, governments must prioritize disaster preparedness initiatives and investments in threat assessments and risk modeling.

The world is experiencing the most abrupt shift in human settlements in history. After decades of rural to urban migration, half of all humanity now lives in cities. By 2050, that figure will surge to 75 percent, with the developing world responsible for most of this increase. Mankind's unprecedented urbanization will create new economic opportunities. But it will also place extraordinary strains on national and munici-

Stewart M. Patrick, "Man-Made Cities and Natural Disasters: A Growing Threat," *Internationalist*, August 14, 2012. Copyright © 2012 by Council on Foreign Relations. All rights reserved. Reproduced by permission.

pal authorities struggling to provide the poor inhabitants of these chaotic agglomerations with basic security, sustainable livelihoods, and modern infrastructure.

And when it comes to natural disasters, today's burgeoning urban centers will increasingly be on the front lines.

Statistics on urbanization are staggering. Cities in the developing world are adding five million residents per month—seven thousand each hour, or more than two per second. For perspective, this is the equivalent to adding one city the size of the United Kingdom every year. Between 2010 and 2050, experts predict, Africa's urban population will triple, while Asia's will double. The vast majority of newcomers are poor. Today, some 828 million people live in slums, including more than 60 percent of city-dwellers in sub-Saharan Africa (and 43 percent in South-Central Asia). By 2040, the global number of slum-dwellers will climb to two billion—nearly a quarter of humanity—as the world's shanty-towns, *bidonvilles*, and *favelas* add another twenty-five million per year.

From a long-term economic perspective, the shift from rural to urban living can be a boon for national wealth. As a general rule, UN HABITAT [United Nations Human Settlements Programme] explains, "The more urbanized a country, the higher the individual incomes."

The concentration of human, physical, and financial capital in cities renders them especially vulnerable to both immediate devastation and lingering disruption to transport, commerce, and communications in the aftermath of major disasters.

Affected Populations and Disasters on the Rise

But the world's rapidly growing cities are increasingly at risk of natural disasters, ranging from catastrophic fires to landslides, massive floods, and tidal waves. This is alarming, given evidence that such events are on the rise. According to the Center for Research on the Epidemiology of Disasters, "the number of people reported affected by natural disasters" rose astronomically between 1900 and 2011, from a few million early in the twentieth century to a peak of 680 million in 2000 (hovering around 300 million today). To be sure, much of this rise is attributable to evolving reporting standards and a growing global population. But alongside these changes has been a growing global awareness of and unwillingness to tolerate the extreme suffering of "natural" disasters.

Moreover, certain types of disasters seem clearly on the rise. Over the last three decades, during which observation techniques have been "fairly comprehensive and consistent," reports of major floods have climbed from an average of less than fifty to just below two hundred per year. Incidences of tropical storms have climbed from around ten to roughly fifteen, and the annual total of U.S. tornadoes and global tsunamis has risen significantly. The financial costs have risen even faster. According to Gerhard Berz, former head of Geo Risks at Munich Re, a German re-insurance corporation, "losses from natural disasters have increased eightfold in economic terms during the last four decades. The insured losses have even increased by a factor of fourteen."

In Houston, Texas, for example, another two decades of urbanization might be enough to double a small thunderstorm's intensity, increasing the risk of flooding.

Beyond the insurance industry, the global business community is increasingly cognizant of the susceptibility of rapidly growing cities to calamity. As the firm Control Risks states in its *RISKMAP 2011*, "The concentration of human, physical, and financial capital in cities renders them especially vulnerable to both immediate devastation and lingering disruption to transport, commerce, and communications in the aftermath of major disasters."

Today's pell-mell urbanization—typically "poorly planned and managed" by local authorities—increasingly occurs in peripheral zones of marginal habitation, leaving hundreds of millions of people at the mercy of natural disasters. Vulnerability is acute along coastal areas, where the strongest population growth is occurring and where "any land remaining available for urban growth is generally risk-prone, for instance flood plains or steep slopes subject to landslides." Of the thirty-three cities predicted to have populations of eight million or more by 2015, Control Risks reports, twenty-one are located in coastal regions. Globally, some one hundred million people live less than one meter above sea level, many in cities like Dhaka [Bangladesh], Lagos [Nigeria], Mumbai [India], New York [New York], Rio de Janeiro [Brazil], and Tokyo [Japan]. Beyond the threat of storms and tsunamis, such low-lying cities are acutely vulnerable to climate-change induced sea level rise.

The confluence of rapid urbanization and natural disasters has been on display many times over the past decade. Haiti's crowded, squalid, capital, Port-au-Prince, surrounded by slopes denuded of trees, suffered repeated, catastrophic flooding even prior to the devastating 2010 earthquake that killed between 200,000 and 250,000 Haitians and caused an estimated $8 [billion] to $14 billion in damage. More recently, disastrous floods in Manila [Philippine capital] were exacerbated by the lack of trees and soil to absorb torrential rainfall.

Hardly Restricted to the Developing World

Vulnerability of urban areas to natural disasters is hardly restricted to the developing world, of course, as the Japanese earthquake [2011] and U.S. experience with Hurricane Katrina [2005] attest. And as any Washington, DC, region resident knows, cities with one million people or more suffer from what meteorologists call the "heat island effect," so that its "annual mean air temperature . . . can be 1.8–5.4°F [Fahrenheit] (1–3°C [Celsius]) warmer than its surroundings." This phenomenon tends to make storms more intense. "In Houston, Texas, for example, another two decades of urbanization might be enough to double a small thunderstorm's intensity, increasing the risk of flooding." Similar dynamics apparently played a role last month [in July 2012], when China suffered its most catastrophic rainstorm in four decades, a deluge that brought sixteen to eighteen inches of rain to some areas, killing thirty-seven people and causing $1.6 billion in damage. Some Chinese researchers attributed the storm's power to the effects of urbanization.

As Ben Franklin's old adage goes, "an ounce of prevention is worth a pound of cure." There are clear steps that governments can take to prepare for disasters, and to increase resilience in their aftermath. Two important steps are building local capacity to anticipate risk levels and establishing channels through which to request resources from state, provincial, or national governments. Another priority is emergency response training in vulnerable cities or neighborhoods. Finally, investing in—and publishing—threat assessments and risk modeling is critical. The United States should seek to catalyze broader global awareness of the threat that natural disasters pose to urban environments, collaborate on disaster prevention efforts around the world, and invest in its own disaster preparedness initiatives.

7

The Increase of
Natural Disasters Is a
Biblical Prophecy

Ron Fraser

Ron Fraser is a columnist for theTrumpet.com, a news website featuring biblically prophetic views and analyses of current events, politics, and society.

Statistics show that natural disasters have drastically escalated since 1990. The most destructive period in recorded history occurred between 2000 and 2009. Over the past ten years, 3,852 disasters caused more than 780,000 deaths, and the trend continues into the current decade. The reason that disasters are increasing is clear and no coincidence: The Bible prophesied that before the return of Jesus Christ to Earth, delayed catastrophic events would be unleashed. Thus, natural disasters and political, economic, and social instability will continue to accelerate until humankind understands them as God's warning sign to an immoral, godless society.

The incidence of natural disaster has risen dramatically over the past 20 years. To close observers of current events in relation to both history and Bible prophecy, this is no mere coincidence. What muddies the water as soon as Bible prophecy is mentioned in relation to natural disaster is the fact that

Ron Fraser, "Why Have Natural Disasters Increased?" theTrumpet.com, February 15, 2013. Reprinted by permission of the Philadelphia Trumpet. For subscription information, visit www.theTrumpet.com or call 1-800-772-8577.

there is a literal abundance of kooks, screwballs and fanatics out there who instantly seize on the latest catastrophe to declare "the end is nigh."

Doomsayers have been doing this for years. Far too many get involved in such activity for personal profit. They peddle their scaremongering by taking advantage of vulnerable people and, for a price, promise to show a way that the gullible can escape the wrath of their god, the next disaster, creatures from outer space, the end of the world, the implosion of the universe or some other such wacky idea. They make it doubly hard for the genuine seeker after truth.

A Trend of Rising and Continuing Natural Disasters

The facts are that statistics prove natural disasters have risen startlingly since 1990. In a law-abiding universe, there has to be a reason for this.

During the 40 years preceding the decade of the 1990s, there were 142 classified natural disasters in the United States. During the 10 years of the 1990s, there were 72. The decade that followed from 2000 to 2009 saw some of the worst and most destructive natural disasters in recorded history across the globe. And the most destructive in terms of loss of life and property? Earthquakes by far!

"'Earthquakes are the deadliest natural hazard of the past 10 years and remain a serious threat for millions of people worldwide as eight out of the ten most populous cities in the world are on earthquake fault lines,' said Margareta Wahlström, UN [United Nations] special representative of the secretary general for disaster risk reduction. . . .

"According to the figures released today by CRED [Center for Research on Epidemiology of Disasters] in Geneva [Switzerland], 3,852 disasters killed more than 780,000 people over the past 10 years, affected more than 2 billion others and cost a minimum of US$960 billion. . . .

"After earthquakes, storms (22 percent) and extreme temperatures (11 percent) were the most deadly disasters between 2000 and 2009. . . . 'The number of catastrophic events has more than doubled since the 1980–1989 decade,' [said] Professor [Debarati] Guha-Sapir, director of CRED" [in a January 2010 press release from the United Nations International Strategy for Disaster Reduction Secretariat].

The current decade has commenced with early indications of that trend continuing. Devastating earthquakes in Haiti and Chile, and record-breaking winter storms in Europe and North America have left many dead and homeless, and town and city infrastructures greatly damaged.

Those prophesied catastrophes were to be a dramatic warning sign to humankind of the sudden, direct, imminent intervention in human affairs by the Creator God Himself!

On reflection, clearly 1989 was a watershed year, a threshold from which natural disasters escalated most dramatically compared to past eras in history.

Why such drastic escalation in natural disasters since 1989—earthquakes, tsunamis, destructive storms, floods, fires, mudslides, extremes of temperatures—which take the figures right off the record charts since statistics have been recorded?

Linking the Facts to Biblical Inerrancy

Well, there is a reason. But it is only apparent to those who, in unbiased, clear-minded fashion, link the facts on the ground with the history of the past and the reality of inerrant Bible prophecies for the future.

There is a prophecy in your Bible that speaks of the world reaching a time when catastrophic events prophesied by humanity's Creator which were once delayed in their fulfillment for a great purpose would no longer be held back by the hand of God. These climactic events were predestined to be delayed in their inevitable fulfillment to allow a great purpose to come to fruition. They were delayed to allow for the good news of His coming Kingdom on Earth to "be preached in all the world for a witness to all nations" before earthshaking events would herald His return (Matthew 24:14). After that, those events would be no longer delayed. A point in time would be reached when they would break out *suddenly* and *dramatically* to SHOCK the world with their *destructive force.* That's the only way God has ever been able to grab the attention of humanity!

It was Jesus Christ Himself, whose death and resurrection many will soon celebrate, who declared that before His return to Earth, "there shall be famines and pestilences and earthquakes in divers places" (Matthew 24:7).

Those prophesied catastrophes were to be a dramatic warning sign to humankind of the sudden, direct, imminent intervention in human affairs by the Creator God Himself! This was to be a warning sign especially to those who ought to know better than to live the prevailing life of immoral, godless profligacy that has so taken over their society today.

Most especially that warning applies to the descendants of the people to whom Jesus Christ personally came 2,000 years ago as a *personal* witness to them of the way humankind was destined by its Creator to live—the people of His very own national human heritage. They remain, though in rapid decline, the most blessed nations on Earth. They are the very descendants of the patriarch Abraham, descendants who rejected Christ's message and slaughtered Him in a most hideous form of death, rather than accept who He was—the literal Son of God. . . .

It was Jesus Christ Himself, whose death and resurrection many will soon celebrate, who declared that before His return to Earth, "there shall be famines and pestilences and earthquakes in divers places" (Matthew 24:7). He went on to declare that additional signs of the closeness of His return would be that His own true and loyal followers would be persecuted at a time of great religious, moral and social confusion.

Why can we point to the year 1989 as the break point, the watershed, from which there have been 20 years of rapidly accelerating incidences of disaster across this world?

Jesus Christ showed the Apostle John, in vision, a keynote prophecy for our day forecasting that we would reach a time when events He had prophesied for our generation would be no longer delayed. Referring to that prophecy, which is contained in Revelation 10, our editor in chief has declared, "We are in a time of no more delay (verse 6), and I believe that is the major reason why our commission has changed from preaching the gospel around the world to prophesying again" (*Prophesy Again: God's Commission to His End-Time Church*).

Act Before Catastrophe Overtakes You

We can prove to any mind open to receive it that the prophesied time of no more delay began on Dec. 7, 1989, just 28 days following the breaching of the Berlin Wall. Ever since that time the world has increasingly destabilized—through accelerating natural disasters, political upheavals, wars and rumors of wars, economic and financial disaster and great moral and social disintegration.

This will continue until humankind gets the message. The message that there is a great omnipresent, omniscient Creator and Sustainer of this universe who has created humankind with an incredible human potential to which he remains blinded by a power which has been set since man's creation on destroying that very same potential!

If you have read this far, then you need to find out just what that potential *is* and really *do* something about *laying hold on it*—FAST—before catastrophe overtakes you and you regret not having acted earlier!

8

Catastrophe on Camera: Why Media Coverage of Natural Disasters Is Flawed

Patrick Cockburn

Patrick Cockburn is an award-winning Irish journalist and foreign correspondent for the Independent.

Media reports of natural disasters are perceived as accurate accounts of the events and devastation. However, this coverage is overwhelmingly deceptive. Regardless of geographical location, similar images and stories of wreckage and dramatic rescues are disseminated, and whether they represent the extremes or norms of a situation is difficult to assess. Cameras pointed at a submerged home, for instance, would not capture normal activity resuming nearby. Furthermore, extreme weather updates, forecasts, and warnings have long become repetitious and predictable in their catastrophic tone and no longer have impact. The media's tendency to exaggerate natural disasters results from the attempts of journalists and reporters to stir an emotional response in their audiences.

The media generally assume that news of war, crime and natural disasters will always win an audience. "If it bleeds, it leads," is a well-tried adage of American journalism. Of the three categories, coverage of war has attracted criticism for its lies, jingoism and general bias. Crime reporting traditionally exaggerates the danger of violence in society, creating an unnecessary sense of insecurity.

Media coverage of natural disasters—floods, blizzards, hurricanes, earthquakes and volcanoes—is, on the contrary, largely accepted as an accurate reflection of what really happened. But in my experience, the opposite is true: the reporting of cataclysms or lesser disasters is often wildly misleading. Stereotyping is common: whichever the country involved, there are similar images of wrecked bridges, half-submerged houses and last-minute rescues.

The scale of the disaster is difficult to assess from news coverage: are we seeing or reading about the worst examples of devastation, or are these the norm? Are victims in the hundreds or the millions? Most usually the extent of the damage and the number of casualties are exaggerated, particularly in the developed world. I remember covering floods on the Mississippi in the 1990s and watching as a wall of cameras and cameramen focused on a well-built house in a St Louis suburb which was slowly disappearing under the water. But just a few hundred yards away, ignored by all the cameramen, a long line of gamblers was walking unconcernedly along wooden walkways to board a river boat casino.

The reporting of natural disasters appears easy, but it is difficult to do convincingly. Over the past year, a series of calamities or, at the least, surprisingly severe weather, has dominated the news for weeks at a time. Just over a year ago, Haiti had its worst earthquake in 200 years, which killed more than 250,000 people. In August, exceptionally heavy monsoon rain turned the Indus river into a vast dangerous lake, forcing millions of Pakistani farmers to flee their homes and take refuge on the embankments. Less devastating was unexpectedly heavy snow in Britain in December and the severe blizzard which struck New York at Christmas. In the first half of January, the news was once again being led by climatic disasters: the floods in Queensland and the mudslides in Brazil.

All these events are dramatic and should be interesting, but the reporting of them is frequently repetitious and dull. This may be partly because news coverage of all disasters, actual or forecast, is delivered in similarly apocalyptic tones. Particularly in the US, weather dramas are so frequently predicted that dire warnings have long lost their impact. This helps to explain why so many people are caught by surprise when there is a real catastrophe, such as Hurricane Katrina breaking the levees protecting New Orleans in 2005 and flooding the city. US television news never admits the role it plays in ensuring that nobody takes warnings of floods and hurricanes too seriously because they have heard it all before.

Governments are warier than they used to be in dealing with disasters, conscious of the political damage they will suffer if they are seen as unfeeling or unresponsive to climatic emergencies. The best-remembered single picture of the New Orleans flood is probably not of water rushing through the streets, but of President Bush peering at it with distant interest out of the window of his aircraft from several thousand feet above the devastation.

Popular response to natural disasters is scarcely an accurate guide to national characteristics.

UK natural disasters are, thanks to the mild climate, not really in the same league as other countries'. Flooding in the Lake District hardly compares with what happened in Brisbane. The same broken or unsafe bridges are filmed again and again. The tone of the reporting is always doleful and, at times, funeral. Worst cases are presented as typical. The pre-Christmas snow and consequent transport difficulties were spoken of as if everybody in Britain spent their entire time longing to get to work instead of welcoming an excuse to stay at home. The simple pleasure of not having to do anything is underplayed and there is never a mention of the fact that the cities and countryside of Britain are at their most beautiful when they are under a blanket of snow.

There is a further difficulty in reporting British disasters, particularly for television and radio. The British still seem, despite some evidence to the contrary, such as in the aftermath of the death of Diana, Princess of Wales, to be genuinely stoical and emotionally tough. It is touching to see reporters baffled and irritated by the refusal of British flood victims, whose living rooms are knee-deep in sewage and water, to treat what has happened to them as more than an unlucky mishap which is not going to ruin their lives.

This British stoicism appears to be quite real even under the most intense pressure. I was in Baghdad in 1990 when British hostages who had been passengers on a British Airways flight that had landed in Kuwait were released just as the Iraqi army was invading. They had then been taken to military camps, power stations, refineries and other Iraqi facilities to deter the US and UK from bombing them. In December that year, Saddam Hussein decided to release his prisoners as a propaganda gesture, the first being freed in front of us journalists in the Al-Rashid hotel in Baghdad. To the frustration of television correspondents and photographers, almost all the former hostages refused to blub to order and seemed impressively unmarked and lacking in self-pity after their ordeal. Television cameras clustered around a single man, evidently drunk, who spoke brokenly of his grim experiences.

Some of the most passionate writing about recent extreme weather episodes in New York and London come not from those who were badly hit but from columnists possibly unaccustomed to inconvenience and discomfort. Philip Stephens wrote an eloquent and bitter piece in the *Financial Times* about the misery of having, after a long flight, to wait an extra three hours in his aircraft at Heathrow because there was nowhere for it to dock. Paul Krugman of *The New York Times* compared the failure of New York's Mayor, Michael Bloomberg, to cope with the blizzard with that of President Bush after Hurricane Katrina. Reminded that some 1,500 people had died in the hurricane and casualties in New York were minimal, he later withdrew the comparison with some embarrassment.

Popular response to natural disasters is scarcely an accurate guide to national characteristics. Other factors may come into play in promoting stoicism and endurance, notably the possession of an insurance policy covering possible damage. After Hurricane Andrew struck south of Miami in 1992, I remember seeing people squatting in the ruins of their wooden houses with large notices telling passing insurance adjusters that the ruined house was still inhabited and they wanted to see him or her. Not surprisingly they were a lot more philosophical about their plight than Haitians in Port-au-Prince or farmers in the Punjab.

Once the initial drama of a disaster is over, coverage frequently dribbles away because nothing new is happening. I remember how bizarre the foreign editor of the newspaper I was then working for found it that I should want to go back to Florida a month after Hurricane Andrew to see what had happened to the victims. "I am not sure that is still a story," he responded sourly to what he evidently considered a highly eccentric request.

Even the worst of disasters has a limited life as a news story unless something new happens.

I could see his point. After a day or two, accounts of disasters sound very much the same. There are the same bemused refugees on the road or in a camp of tents or huts; houses destroyed by an earthquake, be it in Kashmir or Haiti, look like squashed concrete sandwiches; the force of the water in rivers in flood often leaves nothing standing but a few walls and some rubble. Every disaster has uplifting rescue stories when a few survivors are miraculously pulled alive from the wreckage of houses. Refugees always complain, often with reason, about the slow response of their government and the aid agencies.

Even a little looting is reported as a general breakdown of law and order. Post-the Iraq war, most media companies or their insurance companies have contracts with security companies which have every incentive to emphasise the threat to journalists. In Haiti, where the danger was minimal, many correspondents were wearing body armour as if they were on the road out of Kabul.

I have always had sympathy for looters, who are usually just very poor people with every reason to hate the powers that be. I was once in a police station in Haiti that was being systematically torn apart, with looters carefully extracting nails from the woodwork for later sale in the market. They were so good at their work that the stairs collapsed, marooning other looters on the first storey of the police station. I always found in Iraq that the presence or absence of looters is a useful pointer as to how risky a situation really is, since only extreme danger will deter the thieves.

Even the worst of disasters has a limited life as a news story unless something new happens. The Indus floods which started last July were like any great flood, except that their extent was enormous and the waters very slow to subside. In this vacuum of fresh news, spurious reports took life. One claimed that Islamic fundamentalist charities were taking advantage of the failure of the government and Western aid agencies to act and were spreading Islamic militancy among angry and receptive refugees. Journalists liked this story because they know that the suggestion that "Islamic fundamentalist militants" are at work will revive the most dead-in-the-water story in the eyes of a news editor. Islamic militants also promote the tale, and are happy to confirm it, because it shows them as more influential and active than they in fact are.

The story of the Islamic militant charities first emerged during the Kashmir earthquake of 2005 and was widely believed. Eventually, the World Bank, which found that donors were discouraged by the idea that aid was falling into the hands of militants, felt compelled to fund a survey of Kashmiri villagers to disprove the story.

I have always found that the most interesting part of reporting disasters, which brings them to life in my mind, is the way in which they reveal, like nothing else, what a society is really like. I had often been in Miami before Hurricane Andrew struck, but until it was destroyed by the wind and I went to see it, I never realised that there was a sprawling town, its one-storey houses largely made out of wood, to the south of Miami, where workers in the city and in the fruit plantations had their homes. It was not the sort of place that ever appeared in *Miami Vice* or *CSI: Miami*.

Last September, I was in Rajanpur in south Punjab looking at the havoc caused by the Indus floods. I asked how many people had died in one area and was told, as if this was to be expected, that a number of those who had died had been hostages held in their heavily fortified headquarters in the flood plain by local bandits who had manacled them. They had not had time to free them from their chains as the waters of the Indus rose and they had all drowned. It had never occurred to me before, as in Iraq and parts of Afghanistan, that the Punjab had its quota of professional kidnappers and bandits too powerful for the police to deal with.

A central reason why the reporting of natural disasters so often sounds contrived and formulaic is that the journalist feels that he or she must pretend to an emotional response on their own part and that of their audience, which is not really there. It is one thing to feel grief for a single person or a small group whom one knows, but very difficult to feel the same way over the death or misery of thousands one has never met.

I was in Belfast in 1974 at the height of the bombings and sectarian killings. I remember saying to a friend, an MP called Paddy Devlin, that I was shocked by some particularly nasty bomb attack that had killed or mutilated a dozen people. He derided my reaction as spurious. "You don't really feel that," he said. "Nobody who lives here with so many people being shot or blown apart every day can have an emotional reaction to every death. The truth is we don't really feel anything unless something happens to a member of our family or the half-dozen people we are closest to."

9

The Frequency of Earthquakes Is Not Increasing

Colin Stark

Colin Stark is the Lamont Associate Research Professor at the Lamont-Doherty Observatory at Columbia University in New York.

A spate of massive earthquakes—including the devastating quake that hit Japan in March 2011—have occurred early in the twenty-first century, but in geological terms, it is not remarkable. The available geophysical measures prove that seismic activity is not on the rise and tectonic plates, which are behind seismicity, are not in acceleration. However, this is not cause for complacency. As the populations of megacities continue to explode, the threat of earthquakes and tsumanis grow greater. Many are located along fault lines, full of concrete buildings unable to withstand powerful tremors, and lacking in earthquake and tsumani preparedness.

The 21st century is still young, and it has already suffered a spate of catastrophic earthquakes across the world—from Haiti to Chile and New Zealand. The misery continued Friday [March 11, 2011] with an earthquake off Japan so big its seismic waves made the cliffs along the Hudson River [in New York] wobble by almost an inch.

The event was one of the largest ever recorded on seismometers, with the latest estimates from the U.S. Geological Survey putting the magnitude at 9. Only three earthquakes came close to this magnitude during the whole of the 20th century.

Nothing Special

So what's going on?

Geologically speaking, it's nothing special. Seismic activity is not increasing, and the tectonic plates driving all the seismicity are not accelerating—not by any geophysical measure we have at our disposal.

Truly huge earthquakes *seem* to have become more frequent over recent years, partly because their impact on society has risen as vulnerable cities have mushroomed and become more fragile, and partly because of the rarity of gigantic earthquakes and their tendency to cluster for statistical reasons and nothing more. It's a matter of perception and coincidence.

But this does not mean that we should ignore the rising risk of devastating earthquakes along dangerous fault zones in places that have been seismically quiet for a long time, but where increasingly cities have risen.

Only a few weeks ago [in February 2011] Christchurch, New Zealand, was struck by a damaging earthquake of magnitude 6.3, hot on the heels of a larger but less damaging event late last year [2010] of magnitude 7.1 Their magnitudes were rather small compared with the seismic event Friday near Sendai, Japan: The Japan earthquake released roughly 1,000 times more energy more than the first New Zealand quake and 15,000 more than the destructive second.

It's hard to relate the magnitude of an earthquake to how much damage it will do, and it's hard to get a sense of how often earthquakes of different sizes take place.

Earthquakes of magnitudes 6 and 7 are common and largely pass unnoticed by the public because they strike below the oceans, or in remote areas, and cause little to no damage. For example, a magnitude 7.2 earthquake struck offshore Sendai on Wednesday, two days before Friday's event. It was felt in Honshu [island in Japan] but raised few eyebrows in a country used to experiencing minor seismic shaking on a monthly basis.

Seismologists are calling this event a foreshock of the Friday earthquake. It's too bad it wasn't deemed a foreshock until after the main event, but prediction of earthquakes is still a long way off.

No, we should not interpret the recent cluster of destructive earthquakes as a sign that the Earth is cracking up.

Giant earthquakes are indeed rare. Even in countries along the Pacific "Ring of Fire," where tectonic plates are squeezing against each other at inches per year, and gradually storing up more and more elastic energy along big faults, it takes hundreds of years for a jammed fault to reach a point where it will unstick in a magnitude 8 or 9 earthquake. Historical records are never long enough to estimate the average time between events, or to calculate the odds of their reoccurrence with any reliability. Cultural memory is even less reliable.

Risks to Human Populations on the Rise

No, we should not interpret the recent cluster of destructive earthquakes as a sign that the Earth is cracking up. But we should also avoid complacency, because the risk to human populations from earthquakes is undoubtedly on the rise.

Megacities across the world continue to grow, and many are along major faults. Most of these faults have not generated giant earthquakes in recent memory, but historical and geological records, supported by abundant geophysical data, show they do so every few hundred years. For example, along the Himalayan front, a very active fault zone situated between Pakistan, India and Bangladesh lie cities such as Kathmandu, Nepal; Islamabad, Pakistan; New Delhi, India; and Dhaka, Bangladesh.

Most of these megacities have seen their populations swell drastically since the last great earthquake struck. Since then, one- or two-story dwellings built from light materials have been replaced by multistory concrete buildings that are much more dangerous during powerful seismic shaking.

The numbers of people exposed to risk has risen from thousands to millions. None of these megacities or their populations enjoy the remarkable level of earthquake preparedness seen in Japan. Projections of the numbers of fatalities in magnitude 8 events and above reach the terrible levels seen in the Haiti earthquake in January 2010.

Although the recent cluster of catastrophic earthquakes is a coincidence and nothing more, perhaps it will raise awareness of the pressing need to reduce the risk to humans in vulnerable cities across the world.

Tsunami risk is also growing in coastal megacities. Videos of the unstoppable advance of the waves driving through Sendai were a terrifying reminder of a tsunami's power.

There was little damage along the U.S. coasts from this week's events, but memories of the destruction caused by the Sumatra tsunami in 2004 are still fresh.

It is therefore acutely disappointing that House Republicans have proposed cuts in the National Oceanic and Atmospheric Administration budget that would likely lead to furloughs and some closures of the Pacific Tsunami Warning Center in Hawaii.

We should be increasing investment in warning systems and earthquake-tsunami monitoring, not cutting them.

10

Counting the Costs of Calamities

Economist

The Economist *is a weekly British-based publication focusing on international politics and business news.*

Death rates from natural disasters, which are not becoming more common, are on the decline, but their economic costs are spiraling. In 2011 alone, the massive earthquake and tsunami in Japan, flooding in Thailand, and other calamities in New Zealand, Australia, China, and North America cost a record-breaking $378 billion. Despite better disaster preparedness and improved building codes and practices, global populations, economic centers, and manufacturing hubs are becoming more concentrated in vulnerable areas—along coasts, deltas, forests, and fault lines. The trade-offs are most apparent in the developing world, where urbanization helps lift the poor out of poverty, but demolishes natural barriers against disasters and places more people and property in harm's way.

The world's industrial supply chains were only just recovering from Japan's earthquake and tsunami in March when a natural disaster severed them again in October. An unusually heavy monsoon season swelled rivers and overwhelmed reservoirs in northern Thailand. The floodwaters eventually reached Bangkok, causing a political crisis as residents fought over whose neighbourhoods would flood. But before that the economic toll was being felt farther north in Ayutthaya province, a manufacturing hub. The waters overwhelmed the six-metre-high dykes around the Rojana industrial estate, one of several such parks that host local- and foreign-owned factories.

Honda's workers rescued newly built cars by driving them to nearby bridges and hills. The factory ended up under two metres of water and is still closed. Honda was hardly alone: the industrial estates that radiate out from Bangkok are home to many links in the world's automotive and technology supply chains. Western Digital, a maker of computer disk drives which has 60% of its production in Thailand, had two of its factories closed by the floods, sending the global price of drives soaring.

Thailand is no stranger to floods. Europeans once called Bangkok the "Venice of Asia". But rarely have they done so much economic damage. October's deluge cost $40 billion, the most expensive disaster in the country's history. J.P. Morgan estimates that it set back global industrial production by 2.5%.

Such multi-billion-dollar natural disasters are becoming common. Five of the ten costliest, in terms of money rather than lives, were in the past four years. Munich Re, a reinsurer, reckons their economic costs were $378 billion last year, breaking the previous record of $262 billion in 2005 (in constant 2011 dollars). Besides the Japanese and Thai calamities, New Zealand suffered an earthquake, Australia and China floods, and America a cocktail of hurricanes, tornadoes, wildfires and floods. Barack Obama issued a record 99 "major disaster declarations" in 2011.

Acts of God, or Man?

Although deadly quakes are rarely blamed on human activity, it is fashionable to blame weather-related disasters on global warming. It does seem plausible: warm air worsens droughts and lets tropical air hold more moisture, the fuel for cyclones (weather formations that include hurricanes and typhoons). However, a recent study by the Intergovernmental Panel on Climate Change, which represents the consensus among thousands of scientists, expressed little confidence in any link between climate change and the frequency of tropical cyclones.

The world has succeeded in making natural disasters less deadly, through better early-warning systems for tsunamis, better public information about evacuation plans, tougher building codes in quake-prone areas and encouragement for homeowners to adopt simple precautions such as installing tornado-proof rooms in their homes. Annual death tolls are heavily influenced by outliers, such as Haiti's earthquake in 2010 (which killed more than 200,000) or the Bangladeshi cyclones in 1970 (300,000). But, adjusted for the Earth's growing population, the trend in death rates is clearly downward.

The Great Miami Hurricane of 1926, which cost $1 billion in 2011 dollars, would cause $188 billion of damage now.

However, even if natural disasters may be no more common and no more likely to kill people than before, there is no doubt that their economic cost is rising. This is because a growing share of the world's population and economic activity is being concentrated in disaster-prone places: on tropical coasts and river deltas, near forests and along earthquake fault lines.

Thailand is an example of this. Since its last serious floods, in 1983 and 1995, the country's export-oriented industrial base has grown rapidly in the provinces around Bangkok and farther north along the Chao Phraya River. Ammar Siamwalla, a Thai economist, notes that the central plain where many industrial estates now sit was once heavily cultivated for rice precisely because it floods regularly. Although dykes (called levees in America) protect these estates and central Bangkok, they may raise water levels, and thus the risk of flooding, elsewhere.

Wildfires, which destroyed thousands of homes in Texas in 2011 and in Australia in 2009, were more destructive than hitherto because, as populations have grown, new housing has been built in wooded areas. Throughout America's west and south-west, encroaching suburbia has put pressure on forest managers to suppress fires as quickly as possible. Yet repeated fire suppression allows forests to accumulate more fuel which can lead to more intense and devastating fires later on.

Australia's "Black Saturday" bushfires, which killed 173 people and destroyed 2,298 homes in 2009, were said to be the country's worst natural disaster. But a study by Ryan Crompton of Macquarie University and others found that 25% of the destroyed buildings were in bushland and 60% were within ten metres of it, and thus exposed to the threat of fire. The study concluded that if previous fires had occurred with people living so close to the bush as today, a 1939 outbreak of wildfires would have been the deadliest while Black Saturday's would rank second, and only fourth by number of buildings destroyed.

In Harm's Way

America's coasts may be a microcosm of where the world is headed. Florida's population has grown from 2.8m in 1950 to 19m now. Howard Kunreuther and Erwann Michel-Kerjan, disaster experts at the Wharton business school in Pennsylvania, reckon there are now nearly $10 trillion of insured and hurricane-prone assets along the coast from Maine round the Florida peninsula to Texas. Roger Pielke of the University of Colorado at Boulder reckons that the Great Miami Hurricane of 1926, which cost $1 billion in 2011 dollars, would cause $188 billion of damage now.

Whether the economic toll of disasters is rising faster than global GDP is unclear, since a wealthier world naturally has more wealth at risk. Still, the incidence of spectacular, multi-billion-dollar catastrophes seems certain to rise. A 2007 study led by the OECD reckoned that by 2070, seven of the ten greatest urban concentrations of economic assets (buildings, infrastructure and the like) that are exposed to coastal flooding will be in the developing world; none was in 2005. In that time, assets exposed to such flooding will rise from 5% of world GDP to 9%. A World Bank study led by Apurva Sanghi estimated that between 2000 and 2050 the city populations exposed to tropical cyclones or earthquakes will more than double, rising from 11% to 16% of the world's population.

Development by its nature also aggravates risks. As cities encroach on coasts, wetlands and rivers, natural barriers such as mangrove swamps and sand dunes are obliterated and artificial ones—dykes and sea walls—are erected to keep the water out. The result is to put more people and property in harm's way if those barriers fail. After the second world war Japan embarked on a vigorous programme of building sea-walls and dykes to protect its cities against storm surges and tsunamis. That in turn encouraged cities' growth and industrialisation, but for the same reason exposed them to damage if a tsunami overwhelmed their defences, as it did in March.

As a consequence of these skewed incentives, people routinely rebuild in areas that have already been devastated.

As cities on river deltas extract groundwater for industry, drinking and sanitation, the ground subsides, putting it further below sea level and thus requiring even higher dykes. Since 1980 Jakarta's population has more than doubled, to 24m, and should reach 35m by 2020. Land that once absorbed overflow from the city's 13 rivers has been developed, and is now subsiding; 40% of the city is now below sea level.

Perverse Incentives

People originally settled in river deltas precisely because regular flooding made the land so fertile. Those cities have continued to grow because of the natural economic advantages such concentrations of human talent hold for modernising societies. Even when poor people moving to cities know they are increasing their risk of dying in a mudslide or flood, that is more than compensated for by the better-paying work available in cities. And in rich countries, coasts are gaining population simply because people like living near water.

Perverse incentives are also at work. In America, homeowners on floodplains must have flood insurance to get a federally backed mortgage. But federal insurance is often subsidised and many people are either exempt from the rule or live in places where flood risks have not been properly mapped. Some do not buy disaster insurance, assuming they can count on federal aid if their home is destroyed. Once the government declares a disaster, it pays 75–100% of the response costs. Presidents have found it increasingly hard to turn down pleas from local leaders for assistance, especially in election years. Matt Mayer of the Heritage Foundation, a conservative think-tank, says the government routinely takes charge of local disasters that should be well within a state's capability. The result is that state disaster-management atrophies and disaster funding ends up subsidising disaster-prone places like Florida at the expense of safer states like Ohio.

As a consequence of these skewed incentives, people routinely rebuild in areas that have already been devastated. Bob Meyer of the Wharton School gives the example of Pass Christian, a resort town in Mississippi, where an apartment complex was destroyed by Hurricane Camille in 1969, killing 21 people who had taken refuge inside. A shopping centre and condominiums were later built in the same area, only to be wiped out by Hurricane Katrina in 2005, since then more new condominiums have gone up nearby.

This is not all because of incentives. As Mr Meyer says, people have a tendency not to price rare, unpredictable events into their decisions, even if these may have catastrophic consequences. Leo "Chipper" McDermott, the mayor of Pass Christian, notes that more than three decades elapsed between Camille and Katrina. "Life is a chance. And let me tell you something else: water sells."

If human nature cannot be changed, government policy can be. That might mean spending more on preventing disaster so as to cut its costs. Roughly 20% of humanitarian aid is now spent responding to disasters, whereas a paltry (but rising) 0.7% is spent on preventive measures taken to mitigate their possible consequences, according to the World Bank.

A Dutch Rethink

The Netherlands, whose existence has long been at the mercy of nature, may be at the forefront of rethinking how to cope with it. Some 60% of the country is either under sea level or at risk of regular flooding from the North Sea or the Rhine, Meuse and Schelt rivers and their tributaries. In 1953, a combination of a high spring tide and severe storm over the North Sea overwhelmed dykes, flooding 9% of its farmland and killing 1,800 people. The country responded with a decades-long programme of "delta works" to guard estuaries from storm surges, while raising and strengthening dykes.

The success of those defences has, perversely, made the consequences of failure even greater, says Piet Dircke of Arcadis, a Dutch engineering firm specialising in water management. Protected by the delta works and dykes, the land stretching from Amsterdam to Rotterdam has heavily industrialised and now provides most of the country's output. "The northern and southern parts of the Netherlands are far more safe but are economically less attractive. People are moving to the western part of Holland because it's where the economy grows."

In 1993 and again in 1995 heavy river flooding inundated the countryside and nearly rose above dykes in population centres, forcing the evacuation of more than 250,000 people. Katrina was the final wake-up call, making the Dutch face up to both the unreliability of forecasts of once-in-a-century events and the impossibility of their repeating the American feat of evacuating a million people.

The country's philosophy of flood control has as a result pivoted from building ever higher dykes to instead making its cities and countryside more resilient to floodwaters. In 2007 it launched its €2.3 billion "Room for the River" project. At 39 locations along the Meuse, Rhine, IJssel and Waal rivers, dykes are being moved inland, riverbeds deepened and fields now occupied by farms and households deliberately exposed to floods. The Dutch invented the word "polder" centuries ago to describe dry land created by enclosing floodplains (or shallow waters) with dykes. They are now "depolderising", removing or lowering the surrounding dykes and turning land back into floodplains. The Rhine's maximum flow without causing disaster will be raised from 15,000 cubic metres a second to 16,000 and, eventually, 18,000.

The Noordwaard polder south-east of Rotterdam was floodplain until 1973, when the delta works made it suitable for cattle and vegetables. It is now being turned back into floodplain to absorb floodwaters that might otherwise inundate cities upstream. To do so, the government had to persuade 18 farmers to move or have their farmhouses raised. Wim de Wit, who raises 75 cattle on the farm his father started in 1979, chose the latter. Near his farmhouse, earthmoving equipment is building a mound, or "terp," on which a new one will sit, safe from the periodic floods that will follow. It will not be pleasant, Mr de Wit acknowledges, "but it's only once every 25 years." And if he loses any crops or cattle to floods, the government will compensate him.

The Dutch are building an industry of promoting their water-management philosophy around the world. Deltares, a research institute, recommends that the Thai government emulate Room for the River by moving dykes farther back where possible, limiting floodplain development and unifying water management so that safety is no longer subservient to irrigation and electricity generation.

The lesson for poorer countries is that growth is the best disaster-mitigation policy of all.

But the Dutch approach has limits. For one thing it is costly. Farmers were paid market value to leave the polders. To do this in a more densely populated city or industrial area would be prohibitively expensive. In America and China, the government has long had the right to breach dykes and periodically inundate occupied land to relieve extreme flooding. Jaap Kwadijk of Deltares notes that the Dutch government has previously rejected doing the same thing. If a flood comes along that exceeds even the very high designed capacity of the dykes, "we don't have a plan B."

If cities cannot be moved, they must, like the polder farms, be made more resilient to disaster. Rather than rely on dykes to keep water out, Rotterdam is also trying to mitigate the consequences if water comes in. A 10,000-cubic-metre tank was built into a new car park, big enough to catch roughly 25% of the water from a once-in-century flood. A public plaza has been designed to turn into wading pools when it fills with rainwater.

In the city's harbour sits a floating pavilion shaped like three halved footballs built on huge blocks of foam. It is a model for the floating communities the city hopes might one day repopulate the docklands, whose traditional shipping activities are moving elsewhere. Pieter Figdor, one of the pavilion's architects, says floating buildings can be up to seven storeys tall, are inherently floodproof and can easily be moved.

Wealth Protection

Making cities more resilient involves starker trade-offs in the developing world. On the one hand, urbanisation strips cities of their natural defences against disaster and exposes more people to loss of life and property when an earthquake or cyclone hits. On the other hand, urbanisation makes poor people richer. The density and infrastructure of cities makes people more productive and more able to afford the measures needed to keep them safe. So mitigation measures should not discourage people from crowding into vulnerable cities but rather establish incentives for cities and their inhabitants to protect themselves better.

Many cities have tough building codes but fail to enforce them. The World Bank study argues that giving more urban dwellers title to their property would encourage investment in their safety, and lifting rent controls would encourage landlords to comply with building codes, since they could then recoup the cost. Ordinary infrastructure can be designed to double as disaster protection, ensuring that it will be properly maintained when the time comes. Two examples the World Bank gives are schools built on higher ground that double as cyclone shelters and a road tunnel in Kuala Lumpur that doubles as a flood-containment tank.

As societies develop they can afford the human and physical infrastructure needed to protect against, and respond to, natural disaster. In time, last year's earthquake and tsunami and floods will be mere blips in the GDP of Japan and Thailand, thanks to the rapid reconstruction made possible by the same wealth that meant the disasters were so costly to start with. The lesson for poorer countries is that growth is the best disaster-mitigation policy of all.

11

Economic Recovery from Natural Disasters Is Declining

Richard Heinberg

Richard Heinberg is a senior fellow at the Post Carbon Institute and author of eleven books, including The End of Growth: Adapting to Our New Economic Reality.

In many cases, natural disasters have boosted the gross domestic product (GDP), the total value of goods and services a nation produces in a year. Known as the "rebound effect," disaster recovery promotes spending that would not have taken place otherwise. But if a nation faces a disaster of a certain size or conditions that do not support a rebound, its economy will weaken. In 2010 and 2011 alone, a string of earthquakes, floods, and other calamities resulted in significant losses, costing annual GDP growth. A variety of factors—rising populations, urbanization, climate change, and environmental depletion—are inhibiting economic growth, which is necessary to solve or respond to disasters.

Accidents and natural disasters have long histories; therefore it may seem peculiar to think that these could now suddenly become significant factors in choking off economic growth. However, two things have changed.

First, growth in human population and proliferation of urban infrastructure are leading to ever more serious impacts from natural and human-caused disasters. Consider, for example, the magnitude 8.7 to 9.2 earthquake that took place on January 26 of the year 1700 in the Cascadia region of the American northwest. This was one of the most powerful seismic events in recent centuries, but the number of human fatalities, though unrecorded, was probably quite low. If a similar quake were to strike today in the same region—encompassing the cities of Vancouver, Canada; Seattle, Washington; and Portland, Oregon—the cost of damage to homes and commercial buildings, highways, and other infrastructure could reach into the hundreds of billions of dollars, and the human toll might be horrific. Another, less hypothetical, example: the lethality of the 2004 Indian Ocean tsunami, which killed between 200,000 and 300,000 people, was exacerbated by the extreme population density of the low-lying coastal areas of Indonesia, Sri Lanka, and India.

Second, the scale of human influence on the environment today is far beyond anything in the past. . . . The billions of tons of carbon dioxide that our species has released into the atmosphere through the combustion of fossil fuels are not only changing the global climate but also causing the oceans to acidify. Indeed, the scale of our collective impact on the planet has grown to such an extent that many scientists contend that Earth has entered a new geologic era—the *Anthropocene*. Humanly generated threats to the environment's ability to support civilization are now capable of overwhelming civilization's ability to adapt and regroup.

Beyond the Threshhold of Recovery

Ironically, in many cases natural disasters have actually added to the GDP [gross domestic product]. This is because of the rebound effect, wherein money is spent on disaster recovery that wouldn't otherwise have been spent. But there is a threshold beyond which recovery becomes problematic: once a disaster is of a certain size or scope, or if conditions for a rebound are not present, then the disaster simply weakens the economy.

The future GDP costs of climate change are unknowable, but all indications suggest they will be enormous and unprecedented.

Examples of major environmental disasters in 2010 alone include:

- January: a major earthquake in Haiti, with its epicenter 16 miles from the capital Port-au-Prince, left 230,000 people dead, 300,000 injured, and 1,000,000 homeless;

- April–August: the Deepwater Horizon oil rig exploded in the Gulf of Mexico; the subsequent oil spill was the worst environmental disaster in US history;

- May: China's worst floods in over a decade required the evacuation of over 15 million people;

- July–August: Pakistan floods submerged a fifth of the country and killed, injured, or displaced 21 million people, making for the worst natural disaster in southern Asia in decades;

- July–August: Russian wildfires, heat wave, and drought caused hundreds of deaths and the widespread failure of crops, resulting in a curtailing of grain exports; the weather event was the worst in recent Russian history.

But these were only the most spectacular instances. Smaller disasters included:

- February: storms battered Europe; Portuguese floods and mudslides killed 43, while in France at least 51 died;

- April: ash from an Iceland volcano wreaked travel chaos, stranding hundreds of thousands of passengers for days;

- October: a spill of toxic sludge in Hungary destroyed villages and polluted rivers.

This string of calamities continued into early 2011, with deadly, catastrophic floods in Australia, southern Africa, the Philippines, and Brazil.

Without economic growth, we are increasingly defenseless against environmental disasters—many of which paradoxically result from growth itself.

Disastrous Impacts on the GDP

GDP impacts from the 2010 disasters were substantial. BP's losses from the Deepwater Horizon gusher (which included cleanup costs and compensation to commercial fishers) have so far amounted to about $40 billion. The Pakistan floods caused damage estimated at $43 billion, while the financial toll of the Russian wildfires has been pegged at $15 billion. Add in other events listed above, plus more not mentioned, and the total easily tops $150 billion for GDP losses in 2010 resulting from natural disasters and industrial accidents. This does not include costs from ongoing environmental degradation (erosion of topsoil, loss of forests and fish species). How does this figure compare with annual GDP growth? Assuming world annual GDP of $58 trillion and an annual growth rate of three percent, annual GDP growth would amount to $1.74 trillion. Therefore natural disasters and industrial accidents, conservatively estimated, are already costing the equivalent of 8.6 percent of annual GDP growth.

As resource extraction moves from higher-quality to lower-quality ores and deposits, we must expect worse environmental impacts and accidents along the way. There are several current or planned extraction projects in remote and/or environmentally sensitive regions that could each result in severe global impacts equaling or even surpassing the Deepwater Horizon blowout. These include oil drilling in the Beaufort and Chukchi Seas; oil drilling in the Arctic National Wildlife Refuge; coal mining in the Utukok River Upland, Arctic Alaska; tar sands production in Alberta; shale oil production in the Rocky Mountains; and mountaintop-removal coal mining in Appalachia.

Underestimating the Risks and the Damage

The future GDP costs of climate change are unknowable, but all indications suggest they will be enormous and unprecedented. The most ambitious effort to estimate those costs so far, the *Stern Review on the Economics of Climate Change*, consisted of a 700-page report released for the British government in 2006 by economist Nicholas Stern, chair of the Grantham Research Institute on Climate Change and the Environment at the London School of Economics. The report stated that failure by governments to reduce greenhouse gas emissions would risk causing global GDP growth to lag twenty percent behind what it otherwise might be. The *Review* also stated that climate change is the greatest and widest-ranging market failure ever seen, presenting a unique challenge for economics.

The Stern Review was almost immediately strongly criticized for underestimating the seriousness of climate impacts and the rate at which those impacts will manifest. In April 2008 Stern admitted that, "We underestimated the risks . . . we underestimated the damage associated with temperature increases . . . and we underestimated the probabilities of temperature increases." . . .

Colliding with Natural Limits

Declining oxygen levels, acidifying oceans, disappearing species, threatened oceanic food chains, changing climate—when considering planetary changes of this magnitude, it may seem that the end of economic growth is hardly the worst of humanity's current problems. However, it is important to remember that we are counting on growth to enable us to solve or respond to environmental crises. With economic growth, we have surplus money with which to protect rainforests, save endangered species, and clean up after industrial accidents. Without economic growth, we are increasingly defenseless against environmental disasters—many of which paradoxically result from growth itself. . . .

Perhaps the meteoric rise of the finance economy in the past couple of decades resulted from a semi-conscious strategy on the part of society's managerial elites to leverage the last possible increments of growth from a physical, resource-based economy that was nearing its capacity. In any case, the implications of the current economic crisis cannot be captured by unemployment statistics and real estate prices. Attempts to restart growth will inevitably collide with natural limits that simply don't respond to stimulus packages or bailouts.

Burgeoning environmental problems require rapidly increasing amounts of effort to fix them. In addition to facing limits on the amount of debt that can be accumulated in order to keep those problems at bay, we also face limits to the amounts of energy and materials we can devote to those purposes. Until now the dynamism of growth has enabled us to stay ahead of accumulating environmental costs. As growth ends, the environmental bills for our last two centuries of manic expansion may come due just as our bank account empties.

12

International Laws Fail to Address Disaster-Driven Migration

Michael Clemens

Michael Clemens is a senior fellow at the Center for Global Development, a nonprofit think tank that focuses on poverty and inequality.

Their lives ruined by earthquakes, floods, and droughts, more people are crossing international borders. Nonetheless, unlike refugees of war or violence, refugees of natural disasters are not legally allowed entry into other countries. International law must change—the impacts of national disasters often exceed and outlast that of wars. Several possible approaches to addressing disaster-driven migration include extending visa opportunities to displaced populations and reevaluating the allocation of restricted slots of "assisted migration" in destination countries. Still, barriers persist and policies will not likely change without the occurrence of a massive catastrophe.

More and more people cross international borders because their lives have been ruined by an earthquake, flood, drought or hurricane. But they face a black hole of international law. No major migrant destination country allows people legal entry for this reason.

Humanitarian permission maybe given to enter rich countries for other reasons. If violence has ruined your life in the country you live in, you may qualify to enter as a "refugee" or "asylee", as 16% of US immigrants did last year [in 2011]. Equally, if your life was ruined back home by a natural disaster and you enter a rich country without authorisation, many countries won't immediately send you back. But the world has so far decided that the right amount of new, authorised migration because of natural disasters—no matter how horrific—is zero.

Is zero the right number? Think of Haiti. At least 150,000 people died there two years ago [in 2010] when houses and buildings could not withstand a cataclysmic earthquake. Many wars don't have a toll as large, or effects as lasting. The US response was to admit a tiny number of Haitians for emergency medical treatment, and to delay most deportations, but not one Haitian could be admitted to the US because of the disaster. This would have been completely different if war had struck Haiti.

A systematic policy tackling the challenge of post-disaster migration remains far off.

So, what if a limited number of humanitarian entry slots were offered to people affected by natural disaster? How many should it be? And how would it work? There are precedents. For a generation (1952–80), the US unilaterally defined "refugee" to include people fleeing "natural catastrophes", but the provision was almost never utilised. Some other countries have similar de jure provisions today; Sweden, for example, allows for protection of migrants "unable to return to the country of origin because of an environmental disaster". But there is no equivalent of the international refugee system to realise these on-paper mechanisms.

Potential Approaches

One approach is case by case. Over the past year, my colleagues and I have led a successful effort to extend a modest, new visa opportunity to Haitians, explicitly for earthquake relief. Our research, supported by the [John D. and Catherine T.] MacArthur Foundation, showed that migration policy would be a highly effective and inexpensive complement to other US earthquake relief efforts. On this basis, we asked the US government to reverse a ban on Haiti's participation in its largest low-skill work visa programme. The US did so but, most notably, it did so because of the horrific disaster Haiti had just experienced—with bipartisan support, in a bad economy. This step will barely affect overall immigration to the US, but could bring hundreds of millions of new dollars to Haiti at no fiscal cost.

Another approach is to review more systematically how destination countries allocate their limited slots of "assistance" migration. International discussion is under way on how this might be done, but consensus is far off. There is less controversy about giving legal status as "internally displaced persons" to those affected by natural calamity who move domestically. But those crossing borders due to natural events still have no clear legal status anywhere. Many years of discussions in the Inter-Agency Standing Committee and other forums have led to little change. Elizabeth Ferris, Michael Cernea and Daniel Petz have summarised the state of this debate as part of the Brookings-LSE Project on Internal Displacement, a leading voice for reform in this area.

These efforts face political barriers, but our work on Haiti proves such barriers have limits. Admitting humanitarian migrants like refugees isn't a handout, it's an investment. Overall, refugees contribute to the economy at least as much as economic migrants. Great Americans like Intel co-founder Andrew Grove and former secretary of state Madeleine Albright arrived as humanitarian migrants. And the US refugee programme has weathered many economic downturns and political upheavals in its 60-year history.

A systematic policy tackling the challenge of post-disaster migration remains far off. Without a major forcing event such as the humanitarian disasters of the second World War, which gave us modern refugee law, that situation seems unlikely to change. Such a moment might have come for natural-disaster migrants had thousands of Haitians arrived on the shores of Florida after the earthquake, but crushing poverty in Haiti and a US naval blockade put paid to that.

This story is not over, however. With climate change will come the likelihood of increased damage from floods, droughts and hurricanes, especially in the poorest countries. A better migration policy would foresee and accommodate these 21st-century realities, although it might once again arrive too late to prevent initial tragedies.

Organizations to Contact

The editors have compiled the following list of organizations concerned with the issues debated in this book. The descriptions are derived from materials provided by the organizations. All have publications or information available for interested readers. The list was compiled on the date of publication of the present volume; the information provided may change. Be aware that many organizations take several weeks or longer to respond to inquiries, so allow as much time as possible.

Cato Institute
1000 Massachusetts Ave. NW, Washington, DC   20001-5403
(202) 842-0200 • fax: (202) 842-3490
website: www.cato.org

The Cato Institute is an organization dedicated to espousing the libertarian principles of free market economics and limited government intervention in all areas of life. As such, Cato promotes energy and environmental policy that discourages government policies and incentives to push the development of sustainable energy sources, instead advocating for the free market's ability to provide the best solutions to environmental issues such as global warming. On its website, the institute offers articles and commentary on natural disasters.

Disaster Research Center at the University of Delaware (DRC)
166 Graham Hall, Newark, DE   19716
(302) 831-6618 • fax: (302) 831-2091
e-mail: drc-mail@udel.edu
website: www.udel.edu/DRC

DRC conducts field and survey research on group, organizational, and community preparation for, response to, and recovery from natural and technological disasters and other communitywide crises. Its researchers have carried out systematic studies on a broad range of disaster types, including hurricanes, floods, earthquakes, tornadoes, hazardous chemical incidents, and plane crashes. The DRC website provides links to research institutions and information on its own findings.

Earthquake Engineering Research Institute (EERI)
499 14th St., Suite 220, Oakland, CA   94612-1934
(510) 451-0905
website: www.eeri.org

EERI is a national nonprofit technical society of engineers, geoscientists, architects, planners, public officials, and social scientists. The objective of EERI is to reduce earthquake risk by advancing the science and practice of earthquake engineering and improving the understanding of the impact of earthquakes on the physical, social, political, and cultural environment. It also advocates comprehensive and realistic measures for reducing the harmful effects of earthquakes. The institute publishes the *EERI Newsletter* as well as other publications and reports.

Heartland Institute
One S Wacker Dr., #2740, Chicago, IL   60606
(312) 377-4000
website: http://heartland.org

The Heartland Institute's mission is to discover, develop, and promote free market solutions to social and economic problems. The institute promotes common sense environmentalism and presents its ideas on how to best maintain a healthy environment. The site also has an archive of public policy documents and links to their various publications on natural disasters and climate change.

Natural Hazards Center
University of Colorado at Boulder, Boulder, CO   80309-0483
(303) 492-6818

e-mail: hazctr@colorado.edu
website: www.colorado.edu/hazards

The Natural Hazards Center is a national and international clearinghouse of knowledge concerning the social science and policy aspects of disasters. The center collects and shares research and experience related to preparedness for, response to, and recovery from disasters. It publishes the bimonthly newsletter *National Hazards Observer* and electronic newsletter *Disaster Research*. In addition, the center maintains a website of updated information on upcoming conferences and links to publications, organizations, and other Internet resources for hazards research and practice.

United Nations Office for Disaster Risk Reduction (UNISDR)
Palais des Nations, Geneva   CH1211
  Switzerland
+41 229178907-8 • fax: +41 229178964
e-mail: isdr@un.org
website: www.unisdr.org

UNISDR aims to build disaster-resilient communities. Its goal is the reduction of human, social, economic, and environmental losses due to natural hazards and related technological and environmental disasters. UNISDR maintains a library on disaster reduction and selected bibliographies and also a website for the promotion of early warning.

US Centers for Disease Control and Prevention (CDC)
Emergency Preparedness and Response
1600 Clifton Road, Atlanta, GA   30333
(800) CDC-INFO (232-4636)
website: www.bt.cdc.gov/disasters

Preparing people for emerging health threats is one of the CDC's main goals. It contributes to national, state, and local efforts to prepare for and prevent public health disasters before they occur. When a disaster has occurred, the CDC is prepared to respond and support national, state, and local partners in responding in order to improve public health outcomes. After a response to a disaster has ended, the CDC assists in the recovery and restoration of public health functions. Numerous resources are available on its website.

US Federal Emergency Management Agency (FEMA)
US Department of Homeland Security
Washington, DC   20472
(202) 646-2500
website: www.fema.gov

A part of the US Department of Homeland Security, FEMA aims to reduce the loss of life and property and protect the nation from all hazards, including natural disasters, acts of terrorism, and other man-made disasters. FEMA offers a variety of disaster information on its website.

US Geological Survey (USGS) Earthquake Hazards Program
Program Headquarters Office, Reston, VA   20192
website: http://earthquake.usgs.gov

USGS provides scientific information to describe and understand the Earth; minimize loss of life and property from natural disasters; manage water, biological, energy, and mineral resources; and enhance and protect the quality of life. USGS maintains the Earth Science Library and provides podcasts on its website.

Bibliography

Books

Patrick Leon Abbott *Natural Disasters*, 9th ed. New York: McGraw-Hill Higher Education, 2013.

Sandi Doughton *Full-Rip 9.0: The Next Big Earthquake in the Pacific Northwest.* Seattle, WA: Sasquatch Books, 2013.

Paul Farmer *Haiti After the Earthquake.* New York: PublicAffairs, 2012.

John Hannigan *Disasters Without Borders: The International Politics of Natural Disasters.* Malden, MA: Polity Press: 2012.

Donald Hyndman and David Hyndman *Natural Hazards and Disasters.* Belmont, CA: Brooks/Cole, 2010.

Leigh Jones and Rhiannon Meyers *Infinite Monster: Courage, Hope, and Resurrection in the Face of One of America's Largest Hurricanes.* Dallas, TX: PenlandScott Publishers, 2010.

Edward A. Keller and Duane E. DeVecchio *Natural Hazards: Earth's Processes as Hazards, Disasters, and Catastrophes,* 3rd ed. Upper Saddle River, NJ: Pearson Prentice Hall, 2012.

Nancy Mathis *Storm Warning: The Story of a Killer Tornado.* New York: Simon & Schuster, 2007.

Bill McGuire   *Global Catastrophes: A Very Short Introduction.* New York: Oxford University Press, 2009.

Bill Nicoll   *Tsunami Chronicles: Adventures in Disaster Management.* Seattle, WA: CreateSpace, 2013.

Bruce Parker   *The Power of the Sea: Tsunamis, Storm Surges, Rogue Waves, and Our Quest to Predict Disasters.* New York: Palgrave Macmillan, 2010.

Kevin M. Simmons   *Deadly Season: Analysis of the 2011 Tornado Outbreaks.* Boston, MA: American Meteorological Society, 2012.

Mike Smith   *Warnings: The True Story of How Science Tamed the Weather.* Austin, TX: Greenleaf Book Group Press, 2010.

Ted Steinberg   *Acts of God: The Unnatural History of Natural Disaster in America,* 2nd ed. New York: Oxford University Press, 2006.

Jerry Thompson   *Cascadia's Fault: The Coming Earthquake and Tsunami That Could Devastate North America.* Berkeley, CA: Counterpoint Press, 2011.

Periodicals and Internet Sources

Activist Post   "5 Theories Why We're Experiencing
                      Increased Earthquake Activity,"
                      March 19, 2011. www.activistpost
                      .com.

Michael Blanpied   "Seismic Science: Is Number of
                      Earthquakes on the Rise?"
                      Washington Post, March 9, 2010.
                      www.washingtonpost.com.

Axel Bojanowski   "The Disaster Business: Scientists
                      Denounce Dubious Climate Study by
                      Insurer," *Spiegel Online International,*
                      October 23, 2012.

Marlene Cimons   "Perfect Storm: Climate Change and
                      Hurricanes," LiveScience, April 5,
                      2013. www.livescience.com.

Steve Connor   "'Rivers of Rain' to Make Severe
                      Floods Twice as Likely by End of
                      Century," *Independent* (United
                      Kingdom), July 23, 2013.

Stan Cox   "Man-Made Natural Disasters," *Al
                      Jazeera* English, August 4, 2013.

Christina   "Impacts of Hurricane Sandy and the
DeConcini and   Climate Change Connection," World
Forbes Tompkins   Resources Institute, December 2012.
                      www.wri.org.

Amrita Jayakumar   "Choices in Crises," Global Journalist,
                      September 1, 2011. www
                      .globaljournalist.org.

Alyson Kenward   "Increase in Hurricane Numbers Due
                      to Better Detection, Not Climate
                      Change, Study Says," Climate Central,
                      June 17, 2011.

Richard A. Lovett   "Energy Production Causes Big US
                      Earthquakes," *Nature*, July 11, 2013.

Russell McLendon   "Are Hurricanes Linked to Global
                      Warming?" Mother Nature Network,
                      September 13, 2012. www.mnn.com.

Erwann   "Prepare Yourself, Natural Disasters
Michel-Kerjan   Will Only Get Worse," *Washington
                      Post*, September 15, 2011. http://
                      articles.washingtonpost.com.

Andrea Mustain   "Why Has 2011's Tornado Season
                      Been So Terrible?" *Christian Science
                      Monitor*, May 25, 2011. www
                      .csmonitor.com.

Andrea Mustain   "Man-Made Quakes Are Increasing,
                      But May Not Pose Threat," Mother
                      Nature Network, April 21, 2012.
                      www.mnn.com.

*National   "Tsunami Facts in Wake of Japan
Geographic   Earthquake," March 11, 2011.
Daily News*   http://news.nationalgeographic.com.

Andrew C. Revkin   "The #Frankenstorm in Climate
                      Context," *New York Times* blog,
                      October 28, 2012. http://dotearth
                      .blogs.nytimes.com.

Michael Snyder   "Is the Number of Earthquakes Increasing? Why the 5.8 Virginia Earthquake Might Just Be a Preview of Things to Come," The American Dream, August 25, 2011. http://endoftheamericandream.com.

James Taylor   "Don't Believe the Global Warmists, Major Hurricanes Are Less Frequent," *Forbes*, September 5, 2012.

Melia Ungson   "In Sandy's Wake, Millennials Must Take the Lead on Preventing Future Disasters," Next New Deal, March 1, 2013. www.nextnewdeal.net.

Michele Zanini   "'Power Curves': What Natural and Economic Disasters Have in Common," *McKinsey Quarterly*, June 2009. www.mckinsey.com.

Index

A

Acts of God, 69–71
Albright, Madeleine, 86
Ando, Masataka, 8–9
Hurricane Andrew, 60, 62
Anthropocene era, 79
Arcadis, firm, 74
Arctic National Wildlife Refuge, 82
Arctic sea ice, 15
Artz, Kenneth, 27–30
Association of Southeast Asian Nations (ASEAN), 8
Atlantic Multidecadal Oscillation, 21
Australia
    calamity cost in, 69
    El Niño, 21
    flooding in, 69, 81
    infrastructure, 34
    wildfires in, 71

B

Bangladesh, 34, 48, 67
Bernard, Eddie, 8
Berz, Gerhard, 47
Biblical prophecy of natural disasters, 50–55
Bidonvilles, 46
Blizzards, 57, 60
Bloomberg, Michael, 60
Typhoon Bopha, 32, 37
Brazil, 48, 58, 81
Brookings-LSE Project on Internal Displacement, 86

Burnett, H. Sterling, 29, 30
Bushfires, 71

C

Calamities
    acts of God, 69–71
    in harm's way, 71–72
    incentives over, 73–74
    from natural disasters, 68–77
    overview, 68–69
    wealth protection from, 77
Hurricane Camille, 73
Canary Islands, 9
Carbon dioxide emissions, 79
Caribbean, 12–14
Cascadia region earthquake (1700s), 79
Center for Research on Epidemiology of Disasters (CRED), 47, 51
Cernea, Michael, 86
Chao Phraya River, 70
Chernobyl disaster, 41
Chilean earthquake, 9, 52, 64
China, 43, 49, 69, 76, 80
Clemens, Michael, 84–87
Climate change
    acts of God and, 69–71
    disaster risk management, 37
    floods and drought, increasing, 18–26
    floods and drought, not increasing, 27–30
    impact of, 87
    natural disaster severity from, 11–17

overview, 11–12
warmer, higher seas, 12–14
See also Global warming
Coal mining, 82
Cockburn, Patrick, 56–63
Control Risks, 47
Cooperative Institute for Research in Environmental Sciences (CIRES), 10
Crompton, Ryan, 71

D

Deep-Ocean Assessment and Reporting of Tsunamis (DART), 10
Deepwater Horizon disaster, 80, 81–82
Democratic Republic of the Congo, 34
Devlin, Paddy, 63
De Wit, Wim, 75
Dircke, Piet, 74
Dirmeyer, Paul A., 18–26
Disaster-driven migration
    international laws fail to address, 84–87
    overview, 84–85
    potential approaches, 86–87
Disaster risk management, 35–37
Dole, Randall M., 17
Hurricane Donna, 13
Doomsayers, 51
Drought
    defined, 19
    increases in, 18–26
    increasing, 18–26
    not increasing, 27–30
    See also Floods and drought
Dust Bowl (1930s), 21, 42
Dykes (levees), 69–72, 74–76

E

Earthquakes
    foreshock in, 66
    frequency not increasing, 64–67
    magnitudes of, 65–66
    manmade consequences from, 43–44
    media coverage of, 57
    as most destructive, 51
    risk from, 66–67
    See also specific earthquakes
Earth Systems Research Laboratory (ESRL), 17
Economic recovery from natural disasters
    beyond threshold of recovery, 79–81
    as declining, 78–83
    GDP impact, 81–82
    natural limits of, 83
    overview, 78–79
    underestimating risks and damage, 82
Economist (newspaper), 68–77
El Niño/La Niña events, 21
Environment & Climate News (newspaper), 29
Europe, 9, 15, 52, 81
European Centre for Medium-Range Weather Forecasts (ECMWF), 22–23
European Geosciences Union (EGU), 28
Extreme temperatures, 18, 52
Extreme weather
    blizzards, 57, 60
    blocking patterns, 15
    from climate change, 16
    lightning deaths, 18

media opinions on, 59
precipitation, 19, 21–23
rainstorms, 49
reoccurence of, 12
from rising global temperatures, 43
stormy weather, 33–34, 81
thunderstorms, 24, 49
tornados, 10, 18–19, 28–29,
  69–70
trends in, 17, 28
tropical storms, 15, 17, 47
typhoons, 10, 31–32, 37, 70
See also Hurricanes

F

Fault zones, 67
Favelas, 46
Ferris, Elizabeth, 86
Figdor, Pieter, 76–77
Financial Times (newspaper), 59
Floodplains, 28–29, 48, 62, 73–75
Floods and drought
  calamity cost, 69
  damage from, 38
  defined, 19
  dykes and, 69–72, 74–76
  future projections, 22–23
  historical trends, 20–22
  increases in, 18–26, 47
  insurance against, 73
  journalist advocates, 30
  land use decisions questioned,
    28–29
  mechanisms of, 24
  media perceptions, 29–30
  during monsoon season, 68
  not increasing, 27–30
  observational implications,
    25–26
  overview, 18–20, 27

Foreshock in earthquakes, 66
Fortin, Jacey, 31–39
Fossil fuel use, 79
Franklin, Benjamin, 49
Fraser, Ron, 50–55
Freedman, Andrew, 11–17
Fukushima Daini Nuclear Power
  Station meltdown, 7, 40–41

G

Gentle rains, 25
Geophysical Research Letters study,
  28
Geo Risks, 47
Ghesquiere, Francis, 33, 35, 37–38
Global Facility for Disaster Reduc-
  tion and Recovery (GFDRR), 35
Global warming
  alarmists' claims over, 27
  disaster risk management and,
    35–37
  influence of, 43, 69
  as manmade, 12–16, 21
  media responses to, 37–39
  as over-inflated, 30
  overview, 31–33
  stormy weather and, 33–34
  See also Climate change
Grantham Research Institute on
  Climate Change and the Envi-
  ronment, 82
Great Miami Hurricane (1962), 71
Greece, 27–28
Greenhouse gases, 22, 44, 82
Gross domestic product (GDP),
  33, 34, 72, 79, 81–82
Grove, Andrew, 86
Guha-Sapir, Debarati, 52

H

Haiti, urbanization, 48
Haitian earthquake
    cost of, 33
    deaths from, 85
    impact of, 37, 52, 64, 80
    manmade consequences from, 41, 44
    migrants from, 85–86
Hayhoe, Katharine, 13, 16
Heinberg, Richard, 78–83
Heritage Foundation, 73
Hodge, Helen, 34, 36
Hoerling, Martin, 17
Holland, 74
Human activity and natural disasters, 40–44
Humanitarian aid, 74
Hurricanes
    in Atlantic, 14, 36
    climate change and, 87
    deaths from, 19, 60
    disaster-driven migration, 84
    frequency of, 10, 14–15, 69–70
    global warming and, 43
    media coverage of, 57–58
    population growth and, 71
    rebuilding after, 73
    warmer sea temperatures, 12
    See also specific hurricanes
Hussein, Saddam, 59
Hybrid vortex, 15
Hydrologic cycle of Earth, 26
Hydrologic floods, 20

I

India, 48, 67
Indian earthquake, 8
Indonesian earthquake, 7–8, 79

Indus floods, 62
Infrastructure. *See* Urbanization/ urban infrastructure
Inter-Agency Standing Committee, 86
Intergovernmental Panel on Climate Change (IPCC), 14, 19, 22–23, 43
Iraq, 61, 62
Hurricane Irene, 12

J

Japan
    GDP of, 77
    infrastructure, 34
    sea level concerns, 48
    typhoon, 31–32
Japanese earthquake
    cost of, 33
    impact of, 64–65
    overview, 7–9
    preparedness for, 67
Journal of Hydrology, 28
Journal of the American Water Resources Association, 28

K

Kashmir earthquake, 62
Hurricane Katrina
    climate change and, 42–43
    flooding from, 58
    government response to, 60
    manmade influence on, 41
    media hype and, 58
    rebuilding after, 58
    urban vulnerabilities and, 48, 73–75
Krugman, Paul, 60
Kuala Lumpur tunnel, 77

Kunreuther, Howard, 71
Kwadijk, Jaap, 76

L

Land use decisions, 28–29
Lightning deaths, 18
London School of Economics, 82
London's Great Smog (1952), 42
Looters, 61
Love Canal disaster, 41

M

MacArthur Foundation, 86
Macquarie University, 71
Maplecroft, 33–34
Marginal habitation zones, 48
Masson, Doug, 9
Mayer, Matt, 73, 74
McDermott, Leo (Chipper), 74
Mean Lower Low Water, 13
Media coverage of natural disasters, 56–63
Mega-tsunami scenario, 9
Merchant, Brian, 40–44
Messina earthquake, 10
Meteorological events, 17, 20
Michel-Kerjan, Erwann, 71
Migration. *See* Disaster-driven migration
Mudslides, 52, 58, 73, 81
Munich Re, 17, 47

N

Naoto Kan, 7
National Center for Atmospheric Research, 16

National Center for Policy Analysis, 29
National Oceanic and Atmospheric Administration, 16, 28
National Oceanography Centre, 9
National Technical University, 27
Natural disasters
  awareness and, 49
  as biblical prophecy, 50–55
  calamity cost from, 68–77
  climate change and, 11–17
  disaster risk management, 35–37
  economic recovery from, 78–83
  global warming and, 31–39
  human activity and, 40–44
  introduction, 7–10
  media coverage, 56–63
  media coverage of, 57
  overview, 31–33
  responses to, 37–39
  rising trends, 51–52
  urbanization and, 45–49
  See also Economic recovery from natural disasters; Extreme weather
Natural Hazards Risk Atlas, 33
Nepal, 67
Netherlands, 74
New York Times (newspaper), 60
New Zealand, 64, 65, 69
Nigeria, 48
Noordwaard polder, 75
Norcross, Bryan, 15
North Africa, 9

O

Oceanic heat content, 21
Oil drilling, 82

Ong Keng Yong, 8
Overland, James, 16

P

Pacific Decadal Oscillation, 21
Pacific Marine Environmental
  Laboratory, 8
Pacific Tsunami Warning Center,
  67
Pakistani floods, 57, 80
Palmer, Jane, 10
Patrick, Stewart M., 45–49
Petz, Daniel, 86
Philippines
  adverse natural events in, 38
  catastrophic flooding in, 81
  GDP growth and, 34
  seal level concerns, 48
  typhoon in, 32
Pielke, Roger, Jr., 29, 71
Polder, defined, 75–76
Population centers
  death rates from disasters, 70
  extreme weather in, 17, 72–73
  flooding and, 75
  growth of, 33, 44, 46, 79
  polders for, 76
  rise of disasters and, 46–48
  risk to, 66–67
  tsunamis and, 8
  urbanization of, 78–79
  wildfires and, 71
Precipitation
  changes in, 20, 24
  downward trends in, 22
  El Niño effects on, 21
  increases in, 23, 28
  severity of, 19, 25
*Proceedings of the National Acad-
emy of Sciences* study, 14

R

Rainstorms, 49
Reynolds, James, 31
Russian Heat Wave (2010), 43
Russian wildfires, 80

S

Typhoon Sanba, 31–32
Hurricane Sandy, 12–13, 16–17
Sea level
  rise in, 12–14, 37
  urbanization and, 43, 48, 72,
    74
Search engine optimization (SEO),
  41
Sea surface temperatures, 21
Sendai Dialogue, 35
Sendai Report, 36
Seveso disaster, 41
Shale oil production, 82
Shanty-towns, 46
Siamwalla, Ammar, 70
Somalia, 34
Southern Africa, 81
Sri Lankan earthquake, 8
Stark, Colin, 64–67
Stephens, Philip, 59
Stern, Nicholas (Stern Review), 82
Storm chasers, 31
Stormy weather, 33–34, 81
Sub-Saharan Africa, 46
Sumatra tsunami, 7
Sweden, 85
Switzerland, 51

T

Temperature extremes, 52
Texas Tech University, 13
Thailand, 68–69, 76, 77
Thunderstorms, 24, 49
Tornados, 10, 18–19, 28–29, 69–70
Toxic sludge, 81
Trenberth, Kenneth, 42
Trenberth, Kevin, 16
Tropical storms, 15, 17, 47
Tsunamis
    after Japanese earthquake,
      7–8, 33, 38, 68, 77
    danger of, 9–10, 79
    early-warning systems for, 67,
      70
    incidences of, 47, 52
    mega-tsunami scenario, 9
    as preventable, 40
    risk of, 48, 67
Typhoons, 10, 31–32, 37, 70

U

Union Carbide gas leak, 41
United Kingdom (UK), 9, 46
United Nations (UN), 9, 14, 18,
  51
United Nations Human Settle-
  ments Programme (UN
  HABITAT), 46
University of Colorado, 29, 71

Urbanization/urban infrastructure
  affected populations and di-
    sasters, 46–48
  design of, 77
  global concerns, 48–49
  natural disasters and, 45–49
  overview, 45–46
  proliferation of, 78–79
  sea level and, 43, 48, 72, 74
  vulnerabilities, 48, 73–75
  vulnerability of, 32–33
US Geological Survey (USGS), 7,
  28, 65

V

Vietnam, 34
Volcano ash, 81
Volcanoes, 57

W

Water-management philosophy, 76
Water vapor, 24
Watts, Anthony, 29, 30
Wildfires, 18, 71
World Bank, 35–37, 62, 72, 77
World Bank's Disaster Risk Man-
  agement Practice Group, 33
Wynn, Russell, 9

Y

Yemen, 34